LEAD the Charge to Business SUCCESS

A Guide to Starting and Running a Successful Business Based on Lessons Learned at the School of Hard Knocks

ISBN: 0-9747667-0-4

Library of Congress Control Number: 2003099020

Published 2004

Sales & Marketing Professionals Publishing
7695 Watonga Way
Boulder, CO 80303
303-884-7788

Printed in the United States of America

Cover and Interior Design: Andra Keller, Rocks-DeHart Public Relations

Praise for *Lead the Charge to Business Success* from Amazon.com Readers

These reviews appeared on the Amazon website and were not written by other authors in expectation of reciprocal plugs for their books. They came from entrepreneurs and prospective entrepreneurs just like you, people who found the book useful in their business or contemplated business.

★★★★★ **No-Nonsense Advice in Plain Language**, November 30, 2003

A reader from New Orleans, LA—For the beginning entrepreneur or seasoned businessperson, this paperback will give you plenty to think about. The writer candidly describes his mistakes as well as his successes, which I found refreshing. He showed me the common pitfalls facing businesses from their beginnings to their maturities in an organized fashion. I believe that the book will be a resource for me to be kept within arm's reach in the office.

★★★★★ **Review**, September 19, 2003

An Amazon.com Customer—Found this book to be informative, comprehensive, and easy to read. Recommended for anyone thinking of starting their own business. Congratulations to Mr. Hearst for all his success.

★★★★★ **Essential reading for any business owner!**, September 16, 2003

A reader from Scottsdale, AZ—Want to start your own successful business? Buy this book! In fact, buy two copies! I've nearly worn out my first copy from regular use. From a self-assessment review, all the way through growing your business and eventually selling it, everything you need to do it right the first time is here. This book is overflowing with practical details of what to do, and humorous examples of what NOT to do in business from someone who has been there every step of the way. You cannot afford to be without this resource in your business toolkit.

★★★★★ **Buy this book!**, August 21, 2003

A reader from Broomfield, CO—This book is chock-full of helpful and useful information. My copy is highlighted and dog-eared all the way through. It goes from helping you discover if you have what it takes, through preparation and building and growing a business. Every aspect of starting and running a business is discussed so that the reader can be prepared. The author is not only forthright and insightful; he's also entertaining. The practical usefulness of this book makes it well worth the read. Yaahooo!—I'm ready to take the leap!

"The rules of engagement for small businesses have changed forever. It is never more important than now to seek other opinions and new strategies to run and grow your business. This book offers the small business owner a new set of commonsense tools for personal and professional growth—A must-read, particularly if you are starting a business or having trouble growing one."

- William P. Glynn, Vice Chairman, Pearl Street Group, Leading Venture Capital Firm

LEAD the Charge to Business SUCCESS

A Guide to Starting and Running a Successful Business Based on Lessons Learned at the School of Hard Knocks

Jay W. Hearst

Preface

This book is dedicated to the nascent entrepreneur—the person who will be absolutely miserable working for someone else, the person who can find fulfillment only by creating and directing his or her own enterprise. In this book you and I will attempt to help determine whether or not you are that person. If you are, my purpose is to guide you along the path toward achieving that goal.

Included in the dedication are those who have taken the plunge and find themselves asking, "Isn't there anyone out there I can talk to?" Let's talk, friend.

Table of Contents

Introduction

Let's Get Started

Hi. I'm Jay Hearst. Glad to meet you. We're going to get to know each other pretty well over the next few pages. I'd like to start by telling you a bit about me, so that you have a good idea of where I'm coming from. I'll also relate to you some of my business successes and failures. Samuel Smiles once said, "We learn wisdom from failure much more than from success." I'll let you be the judge of that.

This book was not written by a professor of business, nor even by a graduate of one of the better-known business schools. Although I completed an undergraduate degree at Harvard, the only thing I learned there that helped in my later business life was how to find things in the library. These days the Internet has made that task much easier, but you still have to know how to look things up.

I do have an MBA from the largest business school in the country. Guess which one? Wrong! It's SHK, the School of Hard Knocks, and MBA in this case stands for Much Better Attitude.

They say that those who can, do and those who can't, teach. I have "done" and done with some success. While I don't have a teaching degree, I'll try, in this book, to help you in *your* business career by relating some of the things I've done right and a whole bunch of things I've done wrong.

H.G. Wells said, "Wise men learn by other men's mistakes, fools by their own." If you'll let me, I'll try to help you skip a few terms at good old SHK.

What about your part of the bargain? I'm going to be asking you to consider a number of fairly tough questions: Who are you? Where are you? Where do you want to go from here? What are you prepared to do to get there? What do you want to do when you arrive at wherever "there" happens to be? How long will you want to stay? What comes after that? The more honest you can be with yourself, the more likely your success.

As you can guess by its size, this is no coffee table book. Although small, it is not light reading. You will put almost as much effort into reading this book as I did into writing it. But if you're willing to tackle the job, answer the questions, and put some of the ideas we cover into practice, it could make a big difference in your future business *and* personal life.

Most books about starting and running your own business emphasize the "nuts and bolts": where to buy the best copier or how to get bulk prices on envelopes. My principal focus will be on *people*. I don't plan to completely ignore the material aspects: the product, numbers and deals. However, I have come to believe that, if your first concern is the people involved in your business – your associates, employees, customers and vendors – the things seem to work themselves out.

We're going to be talking a lot about leadership. I flinch when I hear someone described as a "manager." I believe you can manage things, but you've got to LEAD people. After this book, you might enjoy reading *Duty First – West Point and the Making of American Leaders* by Ed Ruggero. Whatever your feelings toward the military, you'd find it hard to dispute that it is in the business of training leaders. Many of Ruggero's Academy lessons apply equally well to leadership in business.

A business, any business, is a reflection of its leader or leaders. Great leaders make great businesses. People lacking in leadership skills usually don't last long in business. If, somehow, they do manage to stick around, their companies stagger along from one crisis to another, never making much headway. Whether we're talking about product, sales, customer service, or operations, keep in mind that **someone** has to be up front, carrying the flag. Are you that someone? If you are, whether your title is, or will be—CEO, President, or Owner—your job description is LEADER. We will be talking more about this topic as we go through the book.

In the process of researching and writing this book, I bought and read a number of other books on business and entrepreneurship. With one exception, I found them to be about as dry as Shredded Wheat. You would have thought the authors were discussing the mechanics of lawn mower repair. This was rather puzzling to me. I don't know about you, but I think there's nothing in the world quite as exciting as business. Life is short; why not have a good time while we're living it? "Carpe diem" (seize the day) applies to education, business, and everything else. If something is not rewarding and fun, then why would you bother doing it in the first place, if you had a choice?

The exception to my list of boring books on business was an autobiography by Jack Welch, the former C.E.O. of General Electric. His experience as the head of one of the largest companies in the history of the world might seem a bit different from our day-to-day encounters. However, it's interesting to see how the ups and downs, ins and outs, and do's and don'ts he describes are things we all face. Jack, as he calls himself in the book, commented frequently on the fun he had while doing his job. He agrees with me that work should be fun. By extension, working through *this* book should be enjoyable for you.

That being said, some parts of this book will be more entertaining than others. As an example, business accounting might not get your pulse racing, but it is important to know if you want to succeed in your new enterprise. I expect you may already be familiar with some of the topics we'll discuss here, but you might want to at least skim these and perhaps pick up a new idea or two. You might even disagree with some of my thoughts. That's fine. I'll reluctantly admit that I don't know everything. Shakespeare said, "The fool doth think he is wise, but the wise man knows himself to be a fool."

In other words, it's important to stay open to new ideas. However, let your experience be your guide. If the way you've always done things has worked for you in the past, by all means, stay the course. You can always keep my suggestions in mind as a backup.

By the end of the book I am confident that you will know your business *and* yourself a whole lot better.

Okay, are you ready to get started? I am. Let's go.

"Take This Job and Shove It"

The majority of wage earners have uttered this phrase, or something similar to it, at least once in their working lives. Countless more rehearse this speech over and over in preparation for that moment when they stride into the boss's office because they "just can't take it anymore." In addition, most have thought, at one time or another, that they could "run this damn company better than the boss." This is a natural feeling. Working for other people isn't always the easiest thing to do. As we'll discuss, some people—maybe even you—aren't cut out to work for other people at all. So why isn't everyone starting a business?

The old expression says, "Easier said than done." Almost any view looks better than the one from a windowless cubicle. It's easy for a person to dream. In an ideal world, who wouldn't want to be his or her own boss? The fact is, and I can't overstate this, starting and running your own business is hard, challenging work. Not everyone is up for it. In business, as in marriage, there are good and bad times. Most people fantasize about the good times: the independence, the money, the ego boost. They don't stop to think about the sacrifices, personal and financial, that go into forming and running a company. Would these individuals be able to see their "babies" through the difficult formative years? Maybe. Maybe not.

In a way, it's probably a good thing that not everyone follows through on the dream of telling the boss off. Harvey MacKay has observed that the majority of first-generation millionaires got that way from running their own businesses. These successful entrepreneurs are not run-of-the-mill. Each of them was willing to give it his or her all in pursuit of his or her dream. Not everyone is willing to do this. Should you follow in their footsteps? Read on and see.

What Is This Book?

First and foremost, this book is an Owner's Manual for your new or your current business.

Your car comes with an owner's manual. The alarm clock that wakes you up in the morning comes with an owner's manual. In each of these cases, the manufacturer of this product felt that your experience would be enriched if they were to dedicate a few pages to describing to you how to use their product for maximum satisfaction.

In this owner's manual, we'll be asking you to consider some tough questions. The more honest you can be with yourself, the better. Before you decide whether or not to start or run your own business in the near future, you need to do some serious thinking about the "far future." This is the best time to consider some of the long-range issues that will confront you. Where do you want to be five years from now? How about ten? Twenty? At age sixty-five? Most people are too busy rushing around to take a moment to consider their goals, but this is time well spent. You'd never set off on a trip to unfamiliar territory without a map, would you?

What will you want out of your business when you decide to part with it? Will you have partners to take it over? A spouse? Children? Will you sell out? Merge? Go public? Answering these questions can help you make a solid plan for your future. There's probably little benefit in detailed month-by-month planning for the next twenty years. However, making general goals, both for you and for the business, is critical. Try to imagine how big you'd like your company to be, what type of product you'd like to be making and selling, what effect running your business will have on your family.

This book is also an Owner's Manual for that part of your life spent at work.

Sigmund Freud was once asked what the keys are to living a happy life. His response was quite simply "love and work." The love part is the subject for another book, but, as you've probably guessed, we will be talking quite a bit about work here.

Most people work for a living, and work forms a significant part of their identity. What's the first thing people ask you when you go to a cocktail party? It's "What do you do?" Personally, I think this has become a bit of a cliché, but it is some sort of tribal identification ritual. Like it or not, we are what we do. And it makes sense. Take a twenty-four-hour weekday. Subtract eight hours for sleep and the time you spend eating, clothing yourself, and commuting. Take away those precious hours when you get to do whatever it is you like to do to relax. What do you have left? If you guessed "work," then go to the front of the line. And I'll argue that there's no more demanding or enjoyable aspect of life than starting and running your own business.

There just isn't time in life to do everything you want to do, at least not to do it all well. If it's important to you to spend the bulk of your time with your family and friends or on hobbies, founding a business is probably **not** the best thing for you to do. In a real way, the business will become your family *and* your hobby. The people who work for you will become members of your extended family. If you think this sounds like a big commitment, you're right.

If you start a business, I guarantee that your spouse and the other important people will criticize you for "always thinking about the business" and "putting the business before everything else." Those who have taken the plunge know what I'm talking about. Particularly in the early years, starting and running a business takes a huge amount of time and effort. Think of what it means to be a new parent. An infant, new to the world, needs nearly constant care. It is the same with a new business. If you are not ready to deal with the complaints of your loved ones, you should postpone your endeavor. When a person is interested in joining the clergy, he or she must make a solemn commitment to put aside worldly things in pursuit of a religious life. You'll need to do the same for your business life.

What if you go through this soul-searching and still decide you have to march on? What are the potential rewards for such dedication and sacrifice? Besides the obvious hope of financial gain, there are many others. Probably foremost will be the personal satisfaction of having achieved something significant, either by yourself or with the help of your partners. You'll gain the respect of your peers in the business community. You'll be the boss and get the ego boost that comes from that. Also, you'll get the huge reward of being able to watch your "child" grow and watching the people you've brought on board grow and learn. And, as they say in the infomercial game, "But wait, there's more!" That's not all you'll get for your money.

This book will give you a glimpse of the view from the top. Or at least somewhere near the top. It's all about your perspective. A person at the bottom of a mountain sees it from one angle. The view from the top is quite different. Consider the act of climbing that mountain. Depending on who you are, you might not feel it's worth the time, effort, and money involved in traveling to Nepal just to see Mount Everest. Maybe you feel that a postcard would do the trick. On the other hand, you might decide to journey to Base Camp 1, take a look, and say, "How about that? That sure is a big mountain!" and go home. A third, smaller group of adventurous souls might choose to go further and join an expedition to climb to the summit. Upon reaching it, they might take a moment to consider those who had never come, or who had stopped at the base. They might feel badly for them and the view they missed. The people who decided against the climb, upon hearing the stories, may or may not feel that they had missed out. It's all about perspective.

So it is with business. The vast majority of workers will toil all their working lives at or near the bottom rungs of the ladder, more or less content with their view. Many others advance a certain distance along the "management" path and thus are able to look down at the huddled masses, but they still have to look up to those at the top. And a few reach the pinnacles of success in the corporate world, becoming executive VPs or even CEOs of large, publicly held companies.

And then there are the entrepreneurs, the ones who make it, and the ones who don't. Some start a business only to have it fail or plateau. We could compare them to Everest climbers who fell off the mountain or made it only part of the way up.

Still others try to and succeed in building their own viable businesses, businesses that continue to grow and prosper throughout the work life of the owners. And many of these businesses even outlive their founders. They may be passed on to family members who decide to carry the torch. Or they may be sold or merged, providing capital for descendents and charitable organizations. These are the people who've made it to the top of the mountain.

Who Is This Book for?

This book is for anybody who wants to benefit from forty years of correct and incorrect decision-making.

Learning what *not* to do is at least as important as learning what to do. Now that I'm past seventy, I often think, "Wouldn't it be neat to be able to start over again, with the knowledge and experience I've gained over the past forty years?" Well, I'm not H.G. Wells and I can't go back in time. You, however, can benefit from my experience. And all it costs you is some of your time and the money you shelled out for this book.

This book is for anyone who has to earn a living and would like to be rich some day.

"Rich" is a relative thing. How much is enough? Only you can decide. A person living in a trailer park probably seems rich to a person who is sleeping in the street. In turn, Bill Gates would consider me a pauper. Someone once said, "Money isn't everything, but it's a heck of a lot better than whatever is in second place." Someone else said, "I'd rather be rich and healthy than sick and poor." You will probably agree that in our society it's better to have money. Is a guy driving a Mercedes "happier" than a guy living in a cardboard box under a bridge? Who's to say for sure? They say that money doesn't buy happiness, but I think most of us, given our druthers, would rather be the guy in the Mercedes. It's not all about fancy toys. Don't get me wrong, the toys are nice; but what's even better is being able to provide necessities and a few luxuries for your family. I'd hate not to have been able to provide a decent lifestyle for my children.

As I mentioned earlier, one of the things I've found best about being "comfortable" is the pleasure I get out of giving to good people and good organizations. I have just about as much as I'm going to need, and it's nice to be able to share.

If you want to have more money than you have now, this book can serve as a guide.

This book is for anyone who wants to do his or her own thing.

At the time of your retirement, do you want to be able to look back and sing along with Mr. Sinatra, "I did it my way?" If so, now is the time to start. Doing any job well provides a certain amount of satisfaction. I admire craftspeople who use their hands and their knowledge to make things happen: plumbers, woodworkers, electricians, computer technicians. Many of these folks are artists in their own right. Their artistry usually stems from the unique approach they take to their craft. I imagine setting up a computer network or building a desk would be very gratifying. To me, and probably to you, it's even more gratifying to watch your business grow and prosper.

Unless you plan on keeping your company payroll to one person, you're going to be hiring people along the way. Watching them learn, grow, and mature gave me great pleasure. Having them come back years later and tell me how valuable our association was to them gives me even more.

What This Book Is NOT

This book is not just another get-rich-quick scheme.

If I really wanted to sell a heap of books, I'd title one, "**How to Start Your Own Business and Make a Lot of Money Without Doing Any Work.**" It would sell quickly. I'd be on every talk show. Unfortunately, people who'd bought it and then realized I was full of it would return the book pretty quickly. Despite what you may have heard, there is no such thing as "easy money," the lottery included. If you're looking for a quick, easy path to instant riches, then put this book down and waste your money elsewhere.

This book is not a "coffee table book."

This isn't the kind of book you should leave around to impress people who come over for drinks. This isn't the kind of book you should leave around at all. It can't help you unless you put some effort into it.

Whatever benefit this book can provide, it won't help you if you don't read it, believe it, and work your tail off making your own path to success. To get the most out of it, read it and then keep it on your desk. Refer to it from time to time as you progress in your business.

This book is not overpriced.

Actually, it's a deal. I've billed up to $250 an hour for consulting and as an expert witness. Even at "courtesy" pricing, you'd spend hundreds of dollars in face-to-face consulting to get the information between these covers.

As I've mentioned, I'm currently fairly comfortable from a financial standpoint. I don't really need to worry about how I'm going to pay the rent. I don't need to sweat over how many copies of this book will sell. Most of the royalties received from its sale will go to charity. My purpose in writing the book is to help *you* achieve *your* goals while avoiding some of the pitfalls I encountered.

What's more, if you take away one good idea from reading this book, it's bound to be worth the price you paid many times over.

This book is not a "how-to guide" for producing your particular product or service.

We will assume you had this pretty well in mind before you picked up this book. I'd be hard pressed to do adequate justice to the millions of products and services that are out there.

Let me just pass on a bit of wisdom from my dad. He used to say that if you want to be successful, you need to find a product or service that people need or want, with a production cost that is not easily determined and that customers need to keep replacing.

A good example of successful implementation of this advice is the current ink-jet printer, fax machine, copier, or multi-function device. Various models are now being sold at prices so low that it's difficult to believe the manufacturer can cover the cost of building them. However, at some point they run out of ink, toner, or film. Depending on usage, you could easily spend hundreds of dollars a year for replacements. It's the old story of giving away the razors and selling the blades.

For a while, the manufacturers pretty much had a lock on the replacement-cartridge business. Since then, enterprising entrepreneurs have seized the opportunity to market "generic" cartridges at cut-rate prices, often refilling recycled originals.

I will also assume you have some idea of *why* you feel you will be able to produce and sell this product or service as well as, or better than, anyone else in your market area. We'll be asking you a series of questions later that will test the depth of your resolve on this issue.

What Makes Me Such an Expert? The Story of My Life in Business

This is going to take some time, but I like to think it will be to your benefit.

In 1959, I was working at perhaps the third of the kind of jobs most of us experience right after finishing high school or college. Semi-enthusiastically, I applied for a job as a special agent (aka salesman) with Northwestern Mutual Life Insurance. My brother, Peter, had recently started with Northwestern, was on the fast track, and was very enthusiastic about a career with the company.

At that time, the Chicago General Agent for Northwestern Mutual used an industrial psychologist to interview prospective agents. I received a copy of the report on my session with him, which said, more or less, that I might be better suited for some other profession. I called the psychologist and asked if he might spare a few minutes defining for me what that "other profession" might be. From our conversation, I discovered that finding an opportunity to work for myself was more important to me than serving as an employee.

The word "entrepreneur" was not widely used in those days, and I had no idea about how to go about working for myself. So, it was on to another of "those" jobs. Does this sound familiar?

Four years later, in 1963, I decided it was time to go for it. I quit my job and spent six long, hard months looking at one miserable business after another. It seems that all of them just needed "a young, hardworking person" to transform them overnight from losers to winners. Familiar, again?

Finally, in August 1963, I was put in contact with a Chicago businessman who owned a small company that stocked and sold elastic bandages. Most people refer to them by the trade name, "Ace" bandages. The company, then called The Tetra Company, bought the product from several mills and resold it, under various labels, to hospitals and other healthcare providers. The owner, an attorney, had picked up the business several years prior in pretty much a dormant state. He received it in lieu of legal fees for handling the deceased owner's meager estate.

Tetra was just completing its fiscal year, showing gross revenues of about $100,000 and a net of $5,000. The owner, one of two employees, drew a salary of $15,000.

I was able to structure an arrangement whereby I would purchase one third of the company for $25,000 and would have an option to purchase the remaining two thirds for $50,000 over a three-year period. The owner would remain as president for three years at his current salary and share in the profits up to $25,000.

At that time, selling bandages and other hospital supplies was a fairly straightforward affair. You'd call on the purchasing people or other decision-makers at hospitals, doctors' offices, and clinics, find out their needs and desires, and propose a product that would do the job, hopefully at a saving.

I caught on fairly quickly, and my new partner and I made a game of who could sell the most. The company prospered, and I was able to exercise my option well inside the three-year limit. During this period the company outgrew its rented two-room office and built a modest warehousing building on Chicago's Near North Side. The old owner retired, and several new people were added to the sales and internal staff. Tetra also added other products and built a growing reputation as a distributor of elastic and plastic expendables.

In 1970, Tetra again outgrew its facilities. We purchased and added to a larger building several blocks away. At about this time, the company acquired its first computer system at a cost of $25,000. Our principal requirement for the computer was that it produce a sales report, indicating gross revenue, cost of sales, and gross profit by sales territory, customer, and product. Several computer suppliers scratched their heads over this challenge. Finally one of them managed to cobble together a system, consisting of what would today be called a CPU, a mag-striped ledger-card reader, and two punched-tape readers. The equipment occupied an entire wall of one room of the building. General ledger, accounts payable, accounts receivable, and payroll were byproducts.

One drawback to the system was that each previous month had to be run before the current month's figures could be entered. This was long before the invention of the hard drive. In December, therefore, all eleven preceding months had to pass through, which took almost forty-eight hours – two days and two nights of continuous operation!

By this time Tetra employed a full-time sales manager. Nonetheless, I continued to serve as chief icebreaker, heading north, south, east, and west from Chicago. Among other things, this gave me an excuse to indulge in my hobby of flying light planes. Before each trip a postcard was sent to customers and prospects, featuring a helmeted-and-goggled pilot and the legend "Here Comes the Tetra Man!" This warning postcard enabled the buyers to have their orders ready and piqued the curiosity of new prospects.

Once, while calling on a hospital in Rock Island, Illinois, the purchasing agent said he had to leave the next day for a meeting in Chicago. Asked whether he was driving or flying, he replied that he was taking the bus. I offered him door-to-door Cessna transportation. The offer was accepted and the hospital became a very good customer.

Cleveland, Toledo, Columbus, Indianapolis, Cedar Rapids, Des Moines, St. Louis, Kansas City—each in turn received visits from the "Flying Bandage Salesman." Once a territory was up and running, we hired a sales rep to work it.

And then—Colorado! My wife, Judy, noticed that I had taken to toting skis along on trips to Denver. For some reason, she just couldn't swallow the explanation that "all Colorado salespeople carry skis on their sales calls." What was the big deal about Colorado, anyway?

To try to answer the question, the family scheduled a Christmas-vacation ski trip toVail, and it was love at first flake. We started visiting twice a year and shortly thereafter decided to purchase a condo. We had so much fun in Colorado in the winter that one year we decided to make a summer trip. And that was it. Pretty soon it was, "Pack your stuff; we're moving to Colorado for good." So long to bitter Chicago winds and crippling traffic. Hello to three hundred days a year of sunshine and crystal clear Rocky Mountain air.

We moved to Boulder in July of 1977. This was before the days of telecommuting, and the Internet and I quickly discovered the headaches of trying to run a still-small Chicago business via long-distance phone. I found myself on the plane and back in Chicago much of the time, neglecting my efforts at trying to expand the Colorado/Wyoming territory.

As is the case in the majority of companies, relations between the inside troops and the salespeople at Tetra were less than loving. My absence seemed to exacerbate the situation. On one Chicago trip, the recently hired sales manager offered to buy the business. Hearing this, Connie and Jim Shier, who had been with me for many years and were my chief lieutenants, stated that they were out the door the minute a deal like this was made. They countered with an offer that *they* would buy the business. This seemed like a better plan for several reasons. One, both had been with the company for a number of years and really knew its ins and outs. And, two, they had money accumulated in a company retirement plan while the sales manager didn't.

A deal was quickly struck for a purchase price of $500,000, with about 5 percent to be paid in cash and the balance over eleven years.

Connie and Jim have continued to run Tetra and remain good friends to this day.

For the next couple of years, I jettisoned the nine-to-five routine and ran a trail-riding business, taking tourists on horseback trips in the mountains.

By January 1980, I needed a real job. It is probably not big news to anyone that a 49-year-old with a seventeen-year history of self-employment was not high on anyone's list of ideal candidates for employment. I spent eight long, hard months looking for the right situation.

Being a salesperson, I eventually placed ads in the Denver papers saying, "If you've got it, I can sell it." You wouldn't believe the strange people who answered those ads! One kept talking about credit cards. "Right," I said, "I have one of those."

"No," the man replied, "I'm talking about *processing* credit cards. I want to sell to the people who *accept* the cards, not the ones who use them to make purchases."

I asked, "Where do I fit in?"

After several conversations, I started to figure it out. What he was talking about was indeed selling. You approach a merchant and ask a couple of key questions, "How do you handle the cards now? What do you pay for the service? If I can do it better or the same and save you money, you wanna give me a try?"

And so, Bancard was born.

The original setup in 1980 was rather convoluted—Bancard had an agreement with the aforementioned gentleman, who, in turn, had an agreement with a small bank in Pueblo, Colorado. The bank in Pueblo "sponsored" the arrangement with the Visa and MasterCard organizations. Bancard operated out of my house as "Midtown National Bank–BankCard Division."

The company was capitalized for $3,000. With $700, I bought the company's first piece of equipment, a used IBM Selectric typewriter.

Someone forgot to tell me that the intended customers were small and medium-sized businesses. As soon as I got the hang of it, I headed for the hills and signed the two largest ski areas in Colorado. When ski season started, the charge slips began to arrive in Pueblo in shoeboxes, completely overwhelming the small bank's facilities. It was a disaster waiting to happen.

On February 1, 1981, "it" happened, though from an unexpected direction. The various businesses processing bankcard transactions with Midtown Bank received certified letters canceling the service. The bank would accept no more drafts, and the program was terminated. The first thing my customers did was to call me and ask what the deal was. They had been left out in the cold. I called the bank, only to be told that, since I had no direct agreement with them, no explanation was due to me. The man with whom I did have an agreement was no more helpful and also refused comment. Bancard never got paid for its sales services.

What did I learn from this? My mother used to say, "Lie down with dogs and you get up with fleas." The customers couldn't care less who screwed up; I was the one who sold them on it.

I later found out the story. It appears that Midtown's president, a well-spoken and affable businessman, had for some time been dipping his hand into the bank's funds, to the tune of $1.5 million, a large sum for a small bank. He was convicted, sentenced, and may still be serving time in an Arizona federal prison. For Bancard and me, it was another dead end. And, you guessed it, another six long, hard months, trying to pick up the pieces and get back to work.

In August, I called a bank in St. Petersburg, Florida. This bank signed up businesses for processing by contacting their respective trade associations. Until Midtown's collapse, Bancard/Midtown had successfully competed against this bank for the business of several Colorado associations.

When I explained who I was, what I had been doing and that I had a number of clients that I could win back as customers, the person at the bank said, "Shazam! You're an association! Send 'em in!" and thus Bancard was reborn.

The new process was similar to the old setup, but involved a little more time, patience, and trust on the part of the merchant. "Merchant" is an "inside" term for any business that accepts plastic for payment. The term also encompasses travel agencies, doctors, and airlines, to name a few who might otherwise not consider themselves "merchants."

The merchant now had to mail his charge slips to St. Petersburg and wait ten days before writing a check for the proceeds. What was the reward for this patience and trust? The merchant saved money, often a lot of it. For a business doing $10,000 a month in bankcard business, the reduction in cost could mean an annual savings of up to $1,200 or more, a meaningful sum for a small business.

The pitch took awhile to explain to business owners. It also involved considerable effort to build sufficient trust in our story. Naturally, people were wary. I was talking about their *money*. "Send it to *Florida*?" But, with the potential savings and a growing list of satisfied customers, Bancard was able to grow slowly but steadily. And then, in 1985, something magical happened! The bank we were dealing with in Florida, Landmark Union Bank & Trust, was one of the first in the country to perfect a system called "draft capture." No longer would the merchant have to wait for the mail to deliver the sales slips. He could rent or purchase a terminal, which could read a magnetic stripe on the card. A clerk had merely to slide the card through the terminal, punch in the amount of the sale, and the proceeds would be in the business's checking account the next day. Hallelujah!

What did this mean for the merchant? Low rates *and instant use of funds*. What did it mean to Bancard? The story had gotten easier to tell and profit could be made on the sale or rental of the terminals. Merchants now were extremely receptive to the change. With the ease of sale and the additional income available, recruiting salespeople became very easy, and Bancard, in its still very small way, began to take off.

You're familiar with the expression that "nature abhors a vacuum"? The traditional banks had controlled the Visa and MasterCard associations. They were, by this point, none too fond of Independent Sales Organizations (ISOs), such as Bancard. ISOs had proved to be stiff competition for them. The banks saw the ISOs as hungry wolves circling their cash cow. Visa International and MasterCard International, two separate but nearly identical organizations, owned by their bank members, had established what they termed "interchange" rates. These rates set the cost each bank paid for processing charge-card transactions through the associations. Interchange, at that time, was slightly above 1 percent, and the banks were charging most merchants 3 percent or more. Needless to say, the business had been extremely lucrative before the ISOs arrived to fill the vacuum.

Another tried and true expression goes something like this: "In every garden there dwells a snake." In addition to the legitimate ISOs who had invited themselves to the table, there came along a number of folks whom one of the trade magazines called "The Tin Men." (Remember the movie, starring Danny Divito, about unscrupulous aluminum-siding salesmen?) Two of the most notorious operated out of the Chicago region and did very well for themselves, ripping off everyone in sight—merchants, salespeople, and sponsor banks. A couple of the more enterprising Tin Men began wrongfully appropriating funds belonging to their merchants. They managed to rack up losses for the banks they represented to the tune of over $5,000,000! The bankcard associations held the banks involved responsible for the missing funds, and these sponsor banks had to make good on their ISO's derelictions.

As a result of numerous other scandals, large and small, the associations cracked down on ISOs and their sponsor banks. Some say there was an abortive effort by the associations to force ISOs out of business, but this has never been proven.

A number of ISOs, both legitimate and otherwise, were able to grow faster and outdistance Bancard. Nevertheless, we kept plodding along at a quite satisfactory annual growth rate of 30 - 40 percent.

Banks have historically talked about providing service but have typically come up short when it came time to deliver. As Bancard grew, we began to take over more and more of the customer service functions previously handled by our sponsor banks. We were simply more attuned to the needs of our customers.

Starting in 1989, Landmark began a process of merging with successively larger organizations. Bancard, up to this time considered almost a member of the family, became enmeshed in an ugly turf war. Luckily for us, we had developed a good reputation in the industry and were able to quickly establish relationships with several of the larger, more forward-looking financial institutions.

Somewhere along the line Bancard adopted, as its corporate symbol, the old-fashioned three-legged milking stool. When I grew up in rural Illinois, farmers still milked cows by hand. They sat on small stools having three legs. Presumably this gave greater stability on the uneven floors of cow barns. To us at Bancard, one leg of the stool stood for our customers, the merchants. The second leg represented our vendors and sponsor banks. The third leg stood for Bancard's own people. If you weaken or destroy one leg, what happens? I managed to locate a real milking stool at a nearby antique store and took every opportunity to brandish it aloft.

"The Milking Stool" was also adopted as the name of our in-house newsletter. Many people, myself included, saw this simple philosophy as a major factor in Bancard's ultimate success. We will bring this concept up again in later chapters.

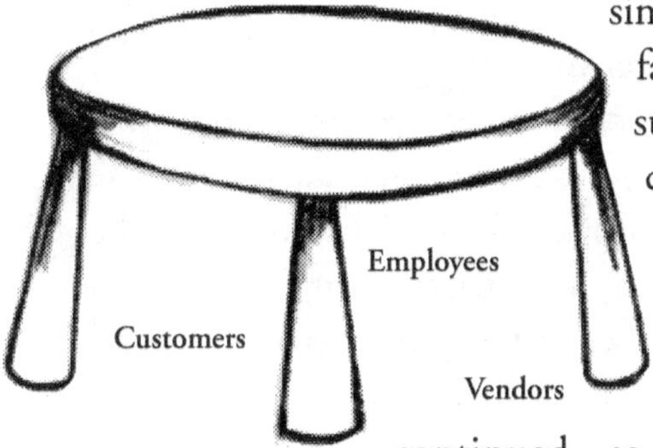

By this time, Bancard was chugging along quite nicely, thank you. Growth continued as before. The sales force numbered around one hundred, and the internal support force was around forty. Every Bancard employee worked on an incentive plan based on his or her performance; the salespeople earned a commission and the internal staff earned a monthly bonus. In most cases, especially with the longer-term employees, the bonus comprised the greater part of their paychecks.

Bancard had progressed from "the kitchen table" to a rented one-room office, to ownership of a small building in Longmont, Colorado. One final move lay ahead. In 1991 we bought and moved to a considerably larger building back in Boulder. This was an impressive office building of 20,000 square feet. We initially occupied the first floor but gradually expanded to take over the whole building.

At our annual sales meeting in January 1997, Paul Martaus, a prominent bankcard industry consultant, predicted that a larger company would swallow up Bancard within the year. This was news to all of us, including the shareholders. I hastened to inform the meeting that there was no such plan in the works, but if for some reason it did happen, Bancard would still be Bancard.

By early summer of that year, we were forced to take notice of the increasing consolidation trend in the industry. One by one, banks and other larger ISOs were acquiring the "old timers" and the multiples were becoming increasingly attractive. Feelers we put out to various players brought very favorable responses. Disregarding the advice of several investment banker "deal makers," we decided to put our own "book" together and try to go it alone. One at a time, the players came to Boulder to make their pitch. One of the discouraging themes we heard was that Bancard was worth more dead than alive. A number of the prospective "partners" wanted the portfolio of merchants but weren't interested in either the company or its people.

People who raise dogs refer to a condition called "kennel blindness." A breeder with kennel blindness places undue faith in the quality of his own dogs. Perhaps we at Bancard suffered from this as well. We felt that if you bought the company, then you bought The Milking Stool—the customers, the vendors and sponsor banks, and most of all, the dedicated sales and inside people.

As it turned out, the party that offered the best price professed agreement with this philosophy. The best price turned out to be listed stock eventually worth around $60,000,000. The deal went forward.

In September of 1997, Bancard was "merged" into PMT Services, Inc., a NASDAQ-listed company. In October of 1998, PMT, in turn, was "merged" into Nova Information Services, Inc, a NYSE-listed company. In the summer of 2001, Nova was "merged" into U.S. Bank. All the shareholders of Bancard came out very well in these transactions. The supervisors and long-term employees received stock options, and the salespeople, thanks to a little foresight on our part, continue to this day to receive residual payments on their accounts.

That was the good news. Our suitors had assured us that we ran the best company in the industry and that there would be no changes. That lasted about a week. After that, the changes came fast and furious. As a direct result, nine months later, the new owners and I agreed that I did not make a very good employee. I was "retired," although they continued to pay off my contract. About two years later, after the second "merger," the Bancard organization was dismantled.

I have no personal gripe. I do feel badly for some of the troops, however. While most received generous stock options, it was sad to see "the family" broken up. Many of us still keep in touch.

And there, for better or worse, you have my story. As you can see, I've been around the block. Hopefully, I've convinced you that I know what I'm talking about.

But enough about me. Now let's start talking about *you.*

Chapter One

Should You Quit Your Day Job?

Those of you who are already in business can skip this chapter if you choose. However, you might enjoy the stories, and you might even find something you didn't know, or had forgotten.

Is starting your own business the path you'd like to explore? There are many rewarding careers that don't involve running a small business. The last thing you want is to put a lot of time, effort, and money into starting a business and then decide, six months or a year later, "I shoulda stayed where I wuz."

Reasons to Keep Your Day Job

Reason # 1: Because you like your steady paycheck

At this point, provided you're currently employed, you can count on payday coming on a regular basis—weekly, bi-weekly, or monthly. You are probably able to budget so that there should always be groceries on the table, perhaps a movie or a night out every week or so, and maybe a family trip to Disneyland once a year.

Unless you are smart, successful and lucky, you won't be able to count on a regular paycheck from your business at first. This could mean months or even years without a steady, predictable income stream. Somehow, there's always one emergency or another, which disrupts the best-laid financial plans.

Reason # 2: Because you like security

Although times change and layoffs happen, most well-established companies offer a degree of security to their employees. Employees of these companies can usually, and I stress *usually*, count on the company—and the job—being there when they get to work in the morning.

There recently have occurred glaring exceptions to the idea that big companies provide security. Ask the people who invested their 401-k money in Enron stock about a large company taking care of them.

Generally speaking, barring luck, brains, and success, small, especially start-up, companies usually can't offer the same degree of security as established companies.

Reason # 3: Because you take comfort in routine

This goes hand-in-hand with security. Many people enjoy the comfort of routine provided by a large company. These people don't mind doing pretty much the same thing, day in and day out. No big surprises, no big decisions.

A small company offers plenty of both: decisions and surprises.

Reason # 4: Because company benefits are important to you

Small startups usually aren't able to offer the same level of employee benefits as their larger, well-established counterparts. If you've grown accustomed to benefits, such as 401-k contributions and paid dental, you'll want to bear this in mind when you make your decision.

Reason # 5: Because you like to take vacations

Most companies give their employees at least two weeks of vacation a year. If taking vacations is important to you, then you might want to keep your day job.

In a startup you can probably forget about getting away for the first few years, other than maybe a long weekend or two. You'll be lucky if you can keep your workweek down to six 12-hour days. Your vacations, if any, will most likely be combined with business trips.

Reason # 6: Because camaraderie is important to you

Like swapping stories around the water-cooler? Look forward to lunch with coworkers and after-work beers with the gang? You'll miss that in your own company. Even as your company grows, things won't be the same. "It's lonely at the top" is not just a saying. Your managers and workers will, hopefully, be friends, but you'll need to keep a command distance. It's really hard to assign unpleasant tasks to, discipline, or, worst case, fire a buddy. Since olden times, military units have had separate rules and facilities for senior officers, junior officers, non-commissioned officers and privates. You won't be ordering your troops into battles, but in a very real way you will hold the power of job life or death over them. You dare not get too familiar with them. This is not to say that you won't be able to have an occasional lunch with them, or even attend the same party. But you'll need at all times to be aware of the how they perceive you, and "good ol' Joe or Jane," their buddy and compatriot, is not the image you want to project.

You will, undoubtedly, make some wonderful friends among your associates and employees, but, always, in the back of your mind, you'll need to consider the impact on your business. It's hard to maintain a friendship when you have to watch everything you say. To avoid putting a crimp in the fun, I generally was the first to depart from company social functions, and I stopped at two drinks or, usually, one.

Reason # 7: Because you don't want too much accountability

You currently accept a certain level of responsibility for your job performance. Odds are, however, your job performance does not determine whether the company lives or dies. This isn't the case when it's your ship. Whether it stays afloat, moves forward, or goes to the bottom will greatly depend on you. Are you the kind of person who can handle this much responsibility?

Reason # 8: Because you don't want to have to worry about feeding other people's children

If your job now involves supervising others, you are aware of the responsibility you have to the people you supervise. Multiply that responsibility tenfold, a hundredfold, or more and you'll understand part of what it means to run a company.

When it's your show, you will assume total responsibility for the financial and, in many cases, the emotional, well-being of your employees. A bad decision or an incorrect action on your part can have a huge effect on their lives and the lives of their families. For an extreme example of a series of bad decisions affecting others, consider Kenneth Lay, former CEO of Enron.

Why You Would Want to Quit Your Day Job

Reason # 1: Because you might make a whole lot of money

Most people start their own business for financial reasons. What they're looking for is money, big piles of it. With the exception of show business, professional sports, top management positions at large corporations, busy surgeons, and some specialized sales positions, ownership of a successful business is practically the only way to make "real money." If you work for someone else for a very long time, and maybe have an advanced degree, you could top out somewhere in the high five or low six figures. And even with one of these high-paying jobs, when you stop working, your income generally stops. Let's face it; a pension and Social Security won't pay for many cruises to the South Pacific when you retire. If you have your eye on the "rock-star money," you'll probably have to cut out on your own. Recurring income from your own business or the proceeds from the sale of it might be your ticket to take those exotic trips and go first class in the bargain.

Reason # 2: Because you'll discover true independence

Are you tired of hearing, "The boss may not always be right, but he's always the boss"? Or, "Yeah, yeah, just do it my way"? Want to get out there and fly with your own wings, blaze your own trail? Want to "do it your way?" It's a great feeling; take it from me.

This may be the greatest reward of starting your own business. Win, lose, or draw, nobody's telling you how to play your cards.

Reason # 3: Because you want to be able to exercise your own creativity—to think outside the box

One phrase I especially hate hearing is, "But we've always done it that way." Someone in a whiney voice holding a half-empty cup of coffee usually utters this phrase. To me, it's one of the ultimate copouts. When I hear it, I respond, "So what? That was then and now is now." The lifeblood of a new business, any business, is new ideas and creative solutions to tough problems.

One of my son's coworkers expressed the encouraging notion that his goal was to "Work as slowly as possible and keep from rocking the boat." This young man was soon let go, but imagine the damage he'd done to company morale.

Are you the type of person who is constantly looking for a better way to do things? Does status quo thinking drive you crazy? Are you tired of hiding your light, or having it turned off by someone with the imagination of a fruit fly? Are you ready to promote yourself from Private or Sergeant to General?

Reason # 4: Because you want to provide opportunity for others to grow

There are few greater kicks in business or in life than inspiring others to "be the best they can be," and then watching them do it.

This is something you will be able to look back on with pride, from the porch of the retirement home. You probably won't remember every deal you cut or every presentation you gave. You will, however, remember how your people made you proud over the years.

With your help they can grow:

- **Professionally**: With coaching and encouragement, they can hone their skills and become ever more valuable to themselves and to the company.
- **Emotionally**: As they develop greater confidence in themselves and take on greater responsibilities, you'll watch them grow and mature as people.
- **Personally**: As they assume greater control over their business lives, this will carry over into their personal lives. They'll develop the skills to think clearly, make their own decisions, and accept responsibility for their actions. Mark my words; these skills will have a profound impact on their family, social, and community relations.

Reason # 5: Because you're looking to do some growing yourself

We've talked about the role you'll play in helping your people become all that they can. But trust me; should you decide to start your own business, you'll be doing plenty of changing and growing yourself.

Reason # 6: Because some people just won't ever be happy working for others

Ask yourself if frustration with your job or with your boss is getting to you. Find yourself short with your friends or coworkers? Do you dread going to work on Monday morning? Do you find yourself complaining more than usual about your "idiot superior"? Going through TUMS by the case?

Human life, according to Hobbes, is "savage, short and brutal." No one would characterize Hobbes as the life of a party. But if you find yourself agreeing with him, maybe it's time for a change.

Reason # 7: Because you're hitting the ceiling at work

Made of glass or otherwise, there is a ceiling in every organization. If you're feeling your head bumping up against something, perhaps it's time for a radical change.

Reason # 8: Because you've been "down-sized"

If that's the case, you've better speed-read this book. Time's a wastin', and you need to do something pretty quickly.

Reason # 9: Because, in spite of laws to the contrary, you keep hearing that you're "over-qualified" or "This job won't provide the challenge you're looking for"

When somebody says this to you, odds are they're really saying, "You're too old, friend. We can hire someone twenty years younger than you who'll be happy with half what you're making." Remember, I started Bancard (the first time) at the age of forty-nine, after I got tired of hearing the man at the state employment office tell me to rewrite my resume for the umpteenth time. I wonder where *he* is today?

Reason # 10: Because you're convinced that you can do it better than anyone else

Are you a good "team player?" You're not? Well, put it there, pal; neither am I. Do you find yourself looking at your watch when meetings drag on and on? Do you find yourself carrying the load while your coworkers congregate at the water fountain? "Lead, follow, or get out of the way." It's your choice.

What Are the Characteristics of a Successful Entrepreneur?

Success is a relative thing. Some people see success as having lots of friends or having a low golf handicap. When it comes to entrepreneurship, the scorecard usually reads in dollars.

So, what are some of the characteristics of a "successful" entrepreneur?

The ability to make quick, gut-level decisions, at least 51 percent of which are right

Don't get me wrong. I believe planning is important. The problem comes when people substitute planning for acting. In a military organization, planners are generally staff people, and they work for commanders. A leader needs to be able to quickly analyze the available information, listen to the alternatives and say, "This way! Follow me!" A leader may do this, or may do that, but will always do *something*. The leader will trust in his or her experience and inner voice.

The ability to lead and inspire others

It is easier to *pull* a rock up a hill than to *push* it up. A leader leads by example. Don't be afraid to get your hands dirty. Some people seem to have more natural leadership ability than others. But I'll argue that almost anyone can do it, if he or she wants to badly enough.

A strong sense of self-confidence

There's a fine line between self-confidence and arrogance. Actually, a leader will strike a balance between arrogance and humility. If you don't believe in yourself, neither will others. You probably don't want to go around constantly claiming you know everything. Loud, pushy people almost always are trying to hide, from themselves and from others, a strong sense of inferiority. And while they may fool themselves, others see right through it. Archimedes said, "Give me a lever long enough, and I shall move the world." In this case, the "lever" is your own sense of self-worth.

I know a person who currently serves as an officer in a non-profit group. This person can't understand why she has trouble getting people to support her projects. As her friend, I have occasionally reminded her that how you ask is at least as important as what you ask. If you have a strong sense of self-confidence, then you don't have to pound the table. A person with a strong sense of self-worth is able to lead and inspire with a soft word, a gesture, and a good example.

Effective communications skills

Remember reading about the man who introduced me to credit-card processing? He was a prime example of a person held back by a difficulty in communicating. This man was intelligent, forward thinking, and way ahead of his time. But he suffered from a severe inability to communicate his ideas to others. He was a total bust at selling and seemed unable to interest others in his ideas. If it weren't for these shortcomings, he might very well have advanced electronic processing of credit cards by at least five years.

A good communicator probably spends 80 percent of the time listening and less than 20 percent of the time talking. Have you ever felt like "you can't get a word in edgewise"? Does this mean that the other person is blabbing on, or does it mean that you are frustrated because you can't do the blabbing? A *really* good communicator has the ability to implant his or her ideas in the minds of others, so that they take ownership of them and carry them out enthusiastically. We will expand on this when we discuss selling, because "selling" and "communicating" are synonyms.

A real test of your communications skills comes when you are in charge of a meeting. There's a saying, "Total time minus meeting time equals production time." Meetings are one way of communicating and have their place. Effective meetings, I mean. Too often, however, meetings consist of the leader preaching, or of each person droning on, in turn, and everyone else staring at their fingertips.

To lead an effective meeting, you need to determine the purpose and the result desired, set the rules down ahead of time, and follow the rules. Each speaker should have something important to contribute or should keep his mouth closed. The leader needs to encourage productive speech and clamp down hard on time wasting.

True concern for others, both inside and outside the company

If all you care about is yourself, others will sense this and will return the favor. On the other hand, they will generally appreciate someone, especially a boss, who exhibits true concern for their welfare. Take the case of a cavalry commander from days of yore. When the company reached camp, a good commander saw that the horses were fed and taken care of, then his men, and, finally, himself.

Not every business is hugely profitable, at least not at first. Many times, the entrepreneur's only reward during the early years will be helping others—his customers, his associates and employees, and his vendors.

A working knowledge of all or most of the skills involved in running a business

These will include, at a minimum: operations, marketing, sales, accounting, and human resources. Much of this knowledge can be gained from schooling or reading. Experience is a far better teacher. If it's a cookie business, then you'd better know (or quickly learn) how to make cookies, sell cookies, and teach others how to make and sell cookies.

At least a rudimentary knowledge of what makes people tick

By definition, a business needs to engage in commerce, the act of buying and selling. Even if you're the only person on the payroll, you'll have suppliers and you'll have customers. A successful businessperson is able to see things from the other person's point of view, to put the shoe on the other foot. Successful business people understand why people do what they do and how to work with others to further their ends and the ends of the business.

And, finally, the willingness to work, work, and then work some more

When you're the boss, you can throw away the time clock. This is especially true in the early years. First off, you won't be able to afford the people you think you need to get the job done. Also, you'd better darn well count on setting an example for your people by being the first in and the last to leave in the evening.

Taking Time Out for Some Thinking

The first and most important part of being reasonably happy and productive is to have an idea of who you are.

The greatest map in the world can't help you find your destination until you first establish where to put the little X, marked "You are here." Up to now, I've been doing all the work—preaching. Now it's time for you to get into the act.

- Who are you?
- Where are you?
- Are you on the right track?
- Are you on *any* track?
- Where do you want to be this time next year?
- In five years?
- In twenty?
- How will you know when you've arrived?
- What things are important to you?
- What people are important to you?
- Will they be important to you in the future?

This would be a great time to put down this book, get out your computer or a little spiral notebook, and put the answers to these questions in writing. Go on, *do it.* Don't just rattle off the answers in your head. Write them. Commit to them. It doesn't matter to if you write them on the back of a shovel with a piece of charcoal. Just write them. I'll be here when you're finished.

You're back already? Want to go back and do a little polishing? Go ahead, this is important. I'll wait.

Okay. Now put that notebook or file in a place where you won't lose it and refer to it at least once a month. Note that it's written on paper, not on stone. You'll want to revise it as you go along. If you wrote that you wanted to earn a million dollars in five years, and you achieved your goal in four, then up the ante a little bit.

Keep the momentum going. Rodin's statue "The Thinker" is just that—a statue. It isn't doing any actual thinking. Some of Satchel Paige's rules for living were, "Keep on jangling," and "Don't look back. Something may be catching up to you."

How many people go through their day-to-day lives without the benefit of self-reflection?

Keep what you wrote in mind as you go through your day. There are too many distractions in the modern world for most of us to take ten minutes to look long and hard in the mirror and figure out whom it is we're staring at. Now that you've done the above exercise (You have done it, haven't you?), you're ahead of most of the people you'll meet during the day. They just drift along, reacting to whatever happens to them, being pushed like a rudderless boat on the ocean. "If you don't know where you're going, you won't know when you get there."

Think of the people you know whom you consider successful and reasonably well adjusted. Ask yourself, "What *makes* them well adjusted?" Odds are they have a good idea of who they are and what makes them tick. Now think of the people you know who seem angry, frustrated, full of complaints. Often you'll hear them, especially if you ask the right questions, say that they don't feel as if they understand their place in the world. You may hear that other people are to blame for their particular situation. Does this make sense to you? It's been my experience that people who spend the majority of their time focused on themselves tend to be unhappy.

Here's a little exercise for you: Think back and try to remember the precise instant in your life when you were most happy and content. Remember what you were doing, who was with you, what was going on in your head. Now, think back and try to remember the exact moment in your life when you were most *un*happy.

Who was your focus on when you were happiest? Chances are it was other people. And whom were you thinking about when you were down in the dumps? Bet it was yourself. What does this tell you? To paraphrase the noted philosopher Forrest Gump, "Happy is as happy does." The time you spend thinking about how to make *other* people's lives better will pay big dividends in the end. This is what I mean by "selfish altruism."

Time spent thinking about how hard you've got it will probably just make you older.

"The Buck Stops Here"

That was Harry Truman's philosophy. He took it so much to heart that he had a sign made for his desk in the Oval Office. Truman never wanted to be accused of "passing the buck," that is, shifting responsibility or blame to someone else. Whatever your opinion of Truman as a president, you will discover, if you read about him, that he told it like it was. He was not afraid to admit an error, and he didn't look around for a convenient scapegoat when something went wrong. The same can be said about two other twentieth-century White House occupants: Jimmy Carter and Dwight Eisenhower. It does not, unfortunately, apply to one of our more-recent presidents, Mr. Bill: "I did not have sex with that woman." Yeah, right.

When your company disappoints, when it lets down one leg of the Milking Stool—a customer, a vendor, or an employee—the offended party might want to know *what* went wrong, but he or she really isn't interested in learning "whodunit." It's your company, your watch, your ship. You are the captain, and you are responsible when the ship hits a rock.

Excuses, even if they happen to be true, just don't cut it. You've heard, "My assistant (or the supplier) must have screwed up." Or even worse, "It's your fault, you stupid customer!" How does that strike you when somebody passes the blame? Does this solve your problem? Does it increase the level of respect you have for this person? Probably not. Usually, all this kind of behavior does is aggravate the situation. When all is said and done, **everything reflects on you**. Who hired this assistant in the first place? Who made the contract with the supplier? No, the correct response is *I* or, *my company*, "screwed up." What can we do to make it right?" This cuts off the recriminations and gets down to fixing the problem.

Taking responsibility also sets a good example for your employees and may help build loyalty in the guilty assistant. Nothing in this process precludes a little "counseling" with the person in question, but you might point out in the process that you covered his or her butt with the customer, vendor or other employees.

How to Fail in Business Without Even Trying

Although it's probably somewhat pessimistic, you will hear that something like two out of three U.S. businesses fail in their first year and four out of five take a dive within five years. Regardless of the actual rate of failure, it really is a jungle out there. There are many ways to screw up your business. We will examine some that I have observed, either close up or, thankfully, from a distance.

Accountants will tell you that the reason most new business fail is **under-capitalization.** This may very well be true. Some of the other reasons are, in no particular order:

1. **Misreading of the market** — There is little or no need for this product or service.
2. **Lack of the requisite business skills on the part of the owner or owners** — Sure, you can sell or cook or make pants, but can you do the books, supervise people, sweep the floors?
3. **Failure of the principals to agree on crucial business issues** — I am currently watching what should be a successful business go down the tubes because the partners, who hold equal interests, cannot agree on vital issues.
4. **Unwillingness of one or more of the partners to do their share of the work or put in the necessary time** — "I've got a life outside this business." Remember, from

your childhood, the story of the little red hen? "Who will help bake the cake?" asked the little red hen. "Not me," said the duck.

Probably everyone working for a wage thinks he or she could run the business better than the boss, "If I only had the chance." Maybe so, but odds are this person makes the comment from his or her couch while the boss is still working in the office, or from a bar stool after having left early. Who goes home last and comes to work first, at least in the early stages of a growing, successful business? Generally it's the boss, and that's the way it should be.

And if the business keeps growing, the boss will probably *still* put the most time in. Even when the boss isn't in the office, he or she is probably still working. "Heavy is the head that wears the crown," said Shakespeare in Richard II.

My favorite place to think is in the shower. Often as not, I rush out, still damp, to work on an idea that came to me while the hot water was running. My second favorite time to think is while I'm on vacation. Many times, I've said to my wife, "Judy, we need to cut this trip short. I've just had an idea and I need to get back to work on it." If the business is to run smoothly, then all of the principals had better agree on what constitutes their fair share of work.

Let's take some time to expand on some of the reasons we've identified.

Businesses fail because of lack of capital

You've all seen the typical ad for a franchise or other business opportunity, the type of ad you might see in the classifieds or in entrepreneur-type magazines. It usually says something like, "Make loads of money in your spare time!" and "How I made $5,000,000 in my first year in business without working!" I really hate to burst your bubble, but that's not exactly how it is. The truth, in most cases, is that small businesses are money pits.

Many years ago, in Wilmington, Delaware, I met and came to know a man named Stanley Budner. Stan had assumed control of his late father's newspaper distribution agency. He expanded the business to include photography sales and service and wholesale drugstore sundries, i.e., everything a drugstore sold, other than pharmaceuticals. His market was the whole DelMarVa Peninsula (Delaware and the eastern parts of Maryland and Virginia). Stanley was running a large, successful business at a time when most people his (and my) age were scrabbling for meager wages. The funny thing about Stanley, however, was that he didn't seem to have a whole lot of disposable income. Sure, he was supporting three daughters and, sure, he did have a nice house outside of Wilmington. But, on Saturday nights, Stanley and his wife ate at the same pizza places Judy and I did and stood in line at the same movies. This always puzzled me.

Over the years, I've run a succession of fairly successful businesses. During this time, I've repeatedly fended inquiries from my spouse to the tune of "Where's the household money this month?" and "Why can't we buy this, that, or the other?" We've never had to sell any of the children to pay the rent, but we certainly didn't live lavishly either. I've since come to understand where Stanley was coming from. It takes capital to run a small business, or any business, for that matter. Lots of capital. My brother, Peter, served three years in the Navy after college. He often speaks in nautical terms. He once compared a business to a ship: It takes a lot of fuel to get it moving and keep it moving, even more as the speed increases, in order to counteract the drag of the water. In a business, that fuel is capital.

I have looked at a number of laboriously written business plans that missed the mark when it came to the subject of capital requirements. It's good, probably essential, to have a business plan. However, attempting to accurately forecast capital requirements into the future may be a fool's errand. I would venture to say that, in almost all start-up situations, **whatever you think you'll need wouldn't be enough.** What you spend will be determined by the amount of cash you have on hand or can raise at the time. If, at any given moment, your needs exceed your cash (or available credit), you'll fail. That's the bitter truth.

Furthermore, sooner or later you'll probably have to give up your day job to shepherd your growing business, but don't count on the business providing anything like a good living anytime soon. Not every business owner has to scrimp and save forever in order to keep the business going. Just don't expect to get rich off of your growing concern, at least not right away. The *real* payoff, in most cases, doesn't come until the business is sold, goes public, or is merged into a larger company.

Businesses fail as the result of misjudgment of market niche

There are many ways to misjudge your market. You can offer a product or service that no one really needs or wants. Or you can jump into waters that already are, or soon will be, too crowded. The big companies spend millions of dollars on market research. My daughter-in-law, Julie, up until the time she retired to become a full-time mom, got paid a lot of money by her clients to conduct this type of research. We're talking megabucks. How can a start-up or small company compete with this type of budget? The startup usually has to rely on the intuition and, yes, luck of the boss. This is one of the things that differentiate the successful entrepreneur from the herd—the ability to zero in on something that the rest of us will line up to buy.

Businesses fail because the principals aren't willing to go out and sell

A good salesperson has the ability to *create* a market where there is none—to differentiate his or her product from the rest. Think of the last major purchase you made: a car, a house, a large appliance. Now you probably could have bought it at a number of different places. So why did you buy it where you did? Somewhere along the line, someone sold it to you, convinced you that you had to have *this* house, *this* BMW, *this* washing machine. I will talk more—a lot more—about salesmanship in this book.

For now, just remember this: Whatever the size of the firm, from a one-person shop to a NYSE-listed company, the CEO is the head salesperson.

Businesses fail because the people involved don't have the requisite skills

What is it you do well in business? If you're going to start or run a small company, the answer had better be, "Everything."

Even if you have the capital to hire an accountant, a sales manager, or a production manager, you had better know enough about each of their jobs to at least determine whether these folks are performing up to snuff. "Human resources" is a big buzzword these days, but what does the term mean? It means finding, keeping, and motivating capable people to share your dream and keep it growing. It also means defining their jobs and knowing enough about the jobs they do to be able to fairly evaluate their performance on an ongoing basis.

Businesses fail because the principals are incompatible

As we've said, about 50 percent of all new businesses fail in their first year. A similar percentage of marriages fail in the first year. Why? Don't expect a pat answer on that one here. As with a failed marriage, the possibility exists that the partners, in each case, didn't know each other as well as they thought they did. They may have had a relationship of one kind or another for some time, but perhaps it wasn't as close as they thought it was, or was based on misunderstandings. It's scary to start something all by yourself, and, even running a successful business, it gets "lonely at the top." But, ask yourself, how well do you really know the person or persons you are considering as partners? How will you function when the going gets tough? It is said that two things can doom a partnership: failure—and success. I can say "Amen" to that. For one reason or another, I have parted ways with several of my business associates under both of the above conditions.

Businesses fail because the people in charge fail to apply the Milking Stool Principle

Remember the three legs? Customers, Vendors, and Employees.

Try this experiment. Go into a small retail store or restaurant and criticize something or recommend a change in the menu. The owner might react as if you just spit on the floor. "This is my store and don't you forget it. Be nice or I won't sell you anything!" Could this be one of the reasons why the business is still small?

Here's another experiment. Ask a sales clerk or other first-line employee what he or she likes best about working where he or she works. I'll bet, in most cases, he or she will have a hard time coming up with a ready answer.

These are some of the reasons small businesses can fail. But these things don't have to happen. The key is to be able to recognize them in **your** business and correct them *before* they become problems. Your small business is like an isolated fort in the wilderness. The attack could come from anywhere, and you'll be in a whole lot better shape if you're prepared for it.

What Can You Do?

There are a number of skills and tasks considered *absolutely essential* for a business, any business, to be successful. Some enterprises will, of course, require additional skills, but this is a place to start. Gather together all of the proposed principals of your business around a table. Place a check mark to signify what you, collectively, consider your level of competence at each skill or task.

Skill/Task

Got It Covered	Reasonably Competent	So-So	Need Help	Completely Clueless
Choosing your partners.				
o	o	o	o	o
Making a business plan.				
o	o	o	o	o
Determining a market for the product/service.				
o	o	o	o	o

Identifying and securing required capital.

o o o o o

Finding a location for your business (one that fits worst-case budget while still allowing for growth).

o o o o o

Legal considerations (both initial and continuing, especially compliance with applicable laws and regulations).

o o o o o

Making/buying/procuring the product or service.

o o o o o

Accounting functions.

o o o o o

Marketing functions.

o o o o o

Sales and sales management.

o o o o o

Support functions, including purchase of supplies and raw materials and delivery of product/service to customers.

o o o o o

Give yourself 10 points for a check in the first box, 8 points for checks in the second box, 6 for the third, 4 for the fourth, and 2 for the fifth. Add the scores for each line and write the total here ___________.

What Can't You Do?

Think you had a pretty good score on the preceding quiz? Here is the list of skills/tasks again. I've included a short job description for each task. Re-score yourself after you've read the job description.

Skill/Task

Got It Covered	Reasonably Competent	So-So	Need Help	Completely Clueless

Choose your partner(s).

No, we're not talking about square dancing here. As I noted previously, this one item is probably your first major decision. If you don't foresee a union "for better or for worse" and for a long time, then you'd better find someone else or go it alone.

o o o o o

Making a business plan.

Your business plan should cover all of the following aspects of the business: It should provide a clear road map of the direction of the enterprise for the next five years, in as much detail as possible. It should deal with best-case and worst-case scenarios and everything in between. While this plan cannot possibly foresee all, or even most, of the future events that will affect the business, it is critical that a plan be in place. Also, it's important that you revise it from time to time, as necessary.

o o o o o

Determining a market for the product/service.

Who and where are your customers? Why will they want or need your product or service? What will they pay for it? Where else can they get it or something like it? Will someone else find it easy to supply it better or cheaper down the road?

o o o o o

Determine and secure capital required

How much will your product or service cost to produce? Raw materials? Equipment? Labor? How much to market? Advertise? Sales force? Packaging and shipping? After-sale support? Facilities rent or purchase? Support and administrative personnel? Insurance? Taxes? Supplies? Will you use your funds, other investors' or borrowed money? Who will you get this money from: family, friends, banks, or the fellow on the corner in the black shirt and white tie, wearing the baseball cap? What will be the cost of borrowing, short term and long term? How and when will the loan be paid back? What security will be required? And you had better be thinking about your worst-case scenario here.

Finding a location for the business.

You'll need a location that fits into your worst-case budget while still allowing for reasonable growth. Should you rent or buy? What about zoning? Will you have money for improvements? What will be the short- and long-term costs?

o o o o o

Legal aspect.

You'll have to consider both initial and continuing costs, especially as they relate to compliance with applicable laws and regulations. You'll locate, interview, and employ competent legal counsel. You'll determine steps necessary to start the business. You'll have to ensure continuing compliance with the laws and regulations, especially those dealing with employment and liability issues. What about insurance: liability, fire & theft, business continuation, key person, etc.?

o o o o o

Employees.

Do you have a plan for hiring, paying, and supervising personnel required at various stages of growth? Have you determined the types and numbers of employees required at various stages of the business? Have you set up personnel policies? Job descriptions? Do you know how you'll advertise for, interview, and hire candidates? Determined pay policies that will dovetail with the interests of the employees and the company and produce the desired results? Legal requirements? Fringe benefits? Bonus plans? Profit sharing? Taxes? Determined the how and why of supervision? Enabled company-wide communication to determine and bolster strengths and head off or quickly solve problems?

o o o o o

Making/Buying/Procuring the product/service.

Conceive, design, produce, and test the product or service from start to finish in the most cost-effective manner, including packaging.

o o o o o

Performing the Accounting function.

Will you do it yourself, if you are trained and experienced, hire an employee, or will you interview and hire an outside bookkeeper and/or accountant, preferably a C.P.A.? How will you work with this professional to set up an accounting system that will clearly and easily allow the control of funds, set up the necessary transactions with suppliers, customers, and others, and give a clear and easily accessible picture of the company's financial progress?

o o o o o

Ongoing marketing.

Advertising, public relations, customer feedback, monitoring of competitors and of the market as a whole.

o o o o o

Sales and sales management.

Do you know how you will maximize the sales of product or service in a cost-effective manner? Will you use in-house sales people? An outside sales force? Your own or manufacturers' reps? Local, regional, or nationwide? Pay plan? Training, initial and ongoing? Supervision? How will you evaluate the sales force, both as individuals and as a group?

o o o o o

Support functions.

These functions could include purchasing of supplies and raw materials and delivery of product/service to customers, bills of materials, vendors, purchasing policies, delivery schedules, warehousing, storage, security, and transportation (in and out).

o o o o o

Again, give yourself 10 points for a check in the first box, 8 for the second box, 6 for the third, 4 for the fourth, and 2 for the fifth. Add the scores for each line and write the total here ___________. Was there a different result this time?

Okay, have you ever considered when boarding an airplane or going into surgery that the pilot or surgeon just had to score 70 on his or her flight test or specialty board exam in order to pass? Perhaps you don't want to think too much about this, especially if you're taking a flight or going into the hospital. In our case, passing is 110, *a perfect score,* and no cheating is allowed. That's right; in order to pass you need a "*Got It Covered*" on *every* question, the second time around. If you and your partners made a check mark in any other column, then you should either bone up on that particular aspect, find someone else to handle that task, or abandon your idea right now. This "someone else" can be either a partner or an employee, but it had better be *someone in whom you have absolute confidence*. You need complete confidence in his or her ability to do the job. You also need to be convinced of his or her unquestioned loyalty to you and to the company. This is potentially a huge trap. We'll have more on loyalty to follow. Each and every one of these tasks is too vital for the survival of the business to just hope that someone is on top of them.

We've reached a **Decision Point**: You can either (1) stop reading, put this book away, and go and be real nice to your boss, or (2) you can keep on truckin'.

If your choice was (2), the good news is that we have some help for you. Let's see if we can't fill in some of those gaps and get your collective score up to where it should be. We'll bet that *no one*—not Bill Gates, not Rupert Murdoch, and certainly not me—could honestly achieve a perfect score on his or her own.

How, then, did Bill, Rupert, and, modestly, I do it? I, for one, found some help. Where? In the library, on the Internet, and, most importantly, from other people. In the following chapters of this book, you and I will address all of these aspects.

CHAPTER TWO

You'll Quit Your Day Job—Preparing to Jump

Choose Your Partner—Will You Still Love Me in the Morning?

Too many of my friends and acquaintances over the years have gone through the unpleasant experience of a divorce. It's been tough on them, but it's been even tougher when children were involved.

I don't have the numbers on how many "business marriages" break up each year, but I'll bet it's plenty. Issues range from family problems to personality conflicts to differing work styles to money problems to…you name it. What I'm saying here is: *Think carefully about who you go into business with.* Talk it over and play "What if?" Try to anticipate every possible circumstance that could affect the business and imagine how each of you would react to it. Have a definite understanding as to who does what, who is responsible for what, and who reports to whom. And, finally, *have a bailout plan,* just in case things don't work out. One good way to handle this is to have a buyout agreement in which a partner who wants to terminate the association can name the price and the other partner can choose whether to "buy" or to "sell." You'll also want to discuss how you'll go about settling any major disagreements. You might specify a mandatory and binding coin toss in the presence of a disinterested witness. Merely knowing that the above are in place can often lead to a quick and amicable resolution of a conflict.

The situation is different when one partner owns the majority of the business. In that case, the majority partner generally gets to make the call. When you have three equal partners, of course, any two can carry the day.

Two things can cause a partnership to sour—first, the business can fail, and second, it can succeed. My history with partners is spotty, at best. Some relationships have been great. Others turned out not so great. Connie and Jim became minority partners in Tetra. I "sold" each of them 1 percent of the company for a dollar each. This facilitated their subsequent buyout and has proved to be a win-win for all. My two cowboy partners in High Country Trails bailed out when things began to go south, accompanied by a certain amount of mutual finger-pointing (pick your finger). All three of my partners in Bancard became millionaires, with an average investment of perhaps $15,000. I'd say they did all right for themselves, wouldn't you? Relations with two of the three are presently somewhere below the frosty level. I have occasional contact with the third partner.

It is tempting to put the blame for these not-so-happy endings on "them." I suspect part of the fault was mine. In the past, I have functioned well in a linear relationship: my boss told me what to do and I told the people who I supervised what to do. I feel I have been less effective in a "committee" environment. I wouldn't go so far as to say, "My mind is made up; don't confuse me with facts," but I do tend to speak up rather forcefully when I believe I'm right.

How 'bout you? Are you a team player, or do you function better as a lone wolf?

As I write this, I am, once again, in the same situation as you, starting over in a new enterprise. A couple of years ago, a year after my "retirement" from Bancard, I received notice from the new owners of the company that my employment contract, including my non-compete agreement, had been cancelled. I got right back in the credit card business, pretty much just to have something to do. I haven't threatened any of the big players in the industry in the interim, but the new business has continued to grow steadily. At a recent vendor's presentation, I met two very nice folks who were just getting started in the business. We agreed to talk and see what we could put together. I asked each of them to bring to the table not only their ideas on how to make the combination work but also what to do if it didn't work—a bailout plan. After considerable discussion, we all agreed to go our separate ways. Sure better to decide that at the beginning.

A number of the relationships have had happier endings. Unity and Saul Franko, my two partners in one of my recent ventures, are among my best friends, as are Connie and Jim Shier. Same goes for Jon and Candy Tate, former competitors in the bankcard business and now my partners in several real-estate ventures. I fully expect the situations to continue that way.

Plan Your Work and Work Your Plan

Where do you want to be this time next year? In five years? Ten? Twenty? Think big; this is the time to let your imagination run wild. Pull out the plan you started in the previous part and let's refine it one more time. The "you," in this case, should involve all those close to you: your prospective partners and, particularly, your immediate family.

Sit down and check over your goals: A bigger house with no mortgage? College and maybe graduate school for your children? A luxury car? A substantial investment portfolio?

Travel? A comfortable retirement? There's no such thing as a too-long list. While this list is not really part of your plan, you should keep it in front of you while you write the formal business plan and then keep it where you can look at it and, possibly, update it periodically.

Okay, finished with your personal goal list? Then let's start with your business goals. The first part will look pretty much like the personal list, except that we're talking now about the company, not you personally. Where do you want to be next year, and so on? Five years out is the generally acceptable limit. A lot can happen in five years, and you'll need to be flexible enough to roll with the punches.

While there are professionals who will write a plan for you, it's a good idea to do it yourself first and then possibly go to a professional for fine-tuning, especially if you will need outside capital, and who doesn't?

There are a number of excellent sources on the Internet to help you with this. Check out the American Express site: www.americanexpress.com. It takes you through the whole process, providing instructions, examples, worksheets, and templates. I couldn't improve on it. Another excellent source is the Small Business Administration (www.sba.gov). In addition to the on-site information, the SBA can provide face-to-face help with your business plan.

Finally, as I have never written a business plan, a sample plan written by friends of mine is included in the Appendix.

Remember, though, unless you've written the plan from scratch, anything you've copied from an Internet site or software is only a "plan for a plan." Make sure your plan is *your* plan. This is important, not only because any potential financing source has already seen hundreds of almost identical canned plans, but for your own benefit. Make *your* plan reflect *your* specific ideas and goals.

If you aren't a numbers person, you will be before you go much farther. Vital parts of your plan will be:

A cash-flow statement – A month-by-month forecast of income and expenses by category

A profit and loss statement – A year-end cash-flow summary

A balance sheet – This is a year-to-year chart of what you have (Assets), what you owe (Liabilities) and the difference, Equity, also called Net Worth (which can be positive or negative)

You will want to project these out for the first three years. If you haven't done this before, then get a book on accounting or get some help. Along with the rest of your business plan, these will form a road map, showing you where you've been and where you're going. You will want to review and revise these estimates as you go along.

Include in your plan a mission statement—a page or less describing what you want to accomplish with your business, including your goals, both short term and long term.

Once you've finished and polished your plan, let me see it. *What makes you think you can do this better than present competition?* **This is probably the most important question I'll ask, and it merits considerable thought on your part.** Just why would people want to pay money to you for your product or service? Okay, in five hundred words or less, convince me. Feel free to use another piece of paper.

Are you still convinced you can do it better than anyone else? Okay, now revise your plan to include what you just put down. Show it to several people whose business judgment you respect but who will not be directly involved in your business. Let them critique it and make any necessary further improvements.

Now organize your plan to include at least the following:

* **Cover Page** — Your cover page doesn't have to be too fancy, but it should be unique, neat, and attractive. The cover page should invite the reader to open the business plan and read more.

* **Table of Contents** — This doesn't need to be more than one or two pages.

* **Executive Summary** — Here you'll cover the high points: The purpose of the business, the people involved, competitive advantages you present, etc. Make sure to keep this brief and concise. You will want to limit the number of people receiving the whole plan to those who will read it and can be helpful to your project. The summary can serve as a "teaser" to gauge people's interest.

* **Additional Key Information** — In these chapters, you'll expand on the summary and can include a description of the business, key personnel and their qualifications, financial projections, marketing plans, and proposed location.

If you don't need financing, can you make do without a plan? Yes, you can. I did, several times. Would I try it again without a plan? I don't think so. Now that I know better, I wouldn't want to press my luck.

Other business writers suggest you live your life by your plan. I'll disagree. A plan is a good thing, but it is only a guide. There are *Planners* and there are *Doers.* A successful business owner needs to spend a lot more time *Doing* than *Planning*. I have known wannabe tycoons to spend years "getting ready." A number of them were still "getting ready" at the time of their retirement.

Your Product—A Better Mousetrap?

In medieval times, sons were pretty well required to follow in their fathers' footsteps. Daughters, on the other hand, were expected to get married, keep house, and raise children. Farmers' sons became farmers, tinsmiths' sons, tinsmiths, and so on. Many family names, especially those of Germanic origin, reflect the original occupations of the forebears. Perhaps the most common is "Smith." Others might include "Shoemaker" and "Schaeffer" (German for shepherd). You could come up with many more.

Our capitalist economy gives us much more choice in our future. The key to success in this economy is that it rewards "value added" at every step of the way. It pays those who extract or produce raw materials or service products: coal miners, farmers, computer programmers. It pays those who refine these materials into more useful forms: steel mills, soybean processors, chemical companies. Manufacturers such as General Motors, General Mills, and Microsoft all do well. And the value chain continues through transportation companies, wholesalers, retailers, restaurateurs, and distributors. Each entity moves the product along on its way, to the stores and other firms that sell to the final consumer, the public or other businesses. Service industries follow a similar path, generally with fewer steps. As long as you can truly add value, someone will pay you. Actually, they will pay for *perceived* value. Value, like beauty, is in the eye of the beholder. There have been many good ideas that went nowhere because they didn't appear valuable to their potential markets. On the other side of the coin, unfortunately, are the many scams and rackets that make money, at least for a while, because they happen to look good to their victims. One horrible present example is the e-mails purportedly coming from someone in Africa trying to get money out of the country. If you will just provide your banking information, they will give you 20 percent of their hundreds of thousands of dollars. Sure, they will! Unfortunately, people are falling for this scam left and right.

You need to decide how *you* and your business can best add value. Remember, you're going to be risking your life's savings, as well as whatever you can borrow. You want to make darned sure the product or service you have in mind has value. In keeping with this thought, I would generally advise you to stick to something with which you are already familiar. Barring this, you should at least aim for something with which you can familiarize yourself quickly and easily.

Don't fall into an all-too-common trap. Many folks believe that, because *they* would want or need a particular product or service, others will, as well. 'Tain't necessarily so, friend. I have been asked to consult for several folks who were contemplating new businesses. In the case of two of these people, I gave them the best advice I could: "Forget it." Naturally, this was not what they wanted to hear at the time. In each case, my consulting assignment didn't last very long.

One idea was a sophisticated dental tool. I was invited to accompany my client to a trade show. There, we found several established companies that were offering comparable products at similar or lower prices than my client would be able to offer; I shook my head and told him to keep his day job. I guess I should be happy that he reimbursed my travel expenses.

Another prospective entrepreneur intended to start a trail-riding business on property he owned. I described our naïve attempt at this business and made him a checklist of some of the things he needed to do. I haven't heard whether he persisted in his idea.

On the plus side, I've consulted with a woman who intends to expand her housecleaning service. She has been doing it on her own but has received more requests for her services than she can perform by herself. We are in the process of getting her on the right track toward hiring and supervising others to handle the overload. This is an example of people being willing to pay (handsomely) for someone else to do something they either don't want to or don't have the time to do. I've recently spoken with a gentleman who feels that he can do well marketing inexpensive motor scooters imported from China. I think he's done his homework and I wish him well. I'm also talking to three people who are considering buying property to start a business providing boarding and training for horses and both day and longer-term care for dogs. They think, and I agree, that they'll derive most of their revenue from the canine side of the business.

For many reasons, I was *very* lucky in choosing Bancard. First, the underlying process for handling credit card transactions was very simple, although it got considerably more complex in later years. Second, we weren't reinventing the wheel. The mechanism for delivering the service was pretty well established, thanks to the previous efforts of the card associations (Visa and MasterCard) and their associated banks. Third, our timing was right. We got in the game just before the explosion of the credit card industry. Fourth, and probably most important, the aforementioned associations and banks were pretty smug and pretty lazy. They had divided the country into little medieval fiefdoms and, being true gentlemen, were reluctant to poach each other's customers. Without competition, they had little or no incentive to "give the suckers (their customers) an even break" either in price or in level of service. This left the field wide open for folks like us.

You, as the prospective business owner, will need to do some mental prospecting on your own. Take time to figure out who's going to want or need your product or service. Where are they? How much of it will they need? What will they be willing and able to pay for it? How will you inform them about you, your product or service, and its advantages? How will you convince them to exchange their hard-earned money for it?

You'll remember I mentioned earlier that you shouldn't be married to your plan. Here's a story about a good plan gone wrong. In 1961, I was working in a department store in Richmond, Virginia. I was managing a sewing machine department for a company that leased space in stores in various cities. When we moved to town, we quickly made friends with Sig and Cissy Gershman. Sig was the assistant manager of the shoe department in the store and about my age.

Sig's passion was bowling. He belonged to a league and could be found at the alley at least one night each week.

Richmond, at that time, was in the early stages of racial integration. The "whites only" signs over the restrooms in the store had just been painted over. Recreational facilities, however, had not caught up. African-Americans wanting to attend the movies had to sit in the balconies, which offered substandard seating and cleanliness. Bowling was out of the question for blacks.

One night, over a game of Canasta, Sig broached an idea he'd had for some time—a bowling alley for black people. I caught his enthusiasm and we began to look into the project. Someone beat us to the idea in Richmond, so we shifted our sights to Petersburg, some thirty miles to the south, where we found the perfect site.

Financing, in this case, was ridiculously easy. We approached the Brunswick Company, who agreed to sell us the equipment on an installment basis. They also found a company willing to buy the land, construct the building, and rent it to us on favorable terms. We raised about $20,000 for starting capital from friends and relatives and got the ball, so to speak, rolling.

As construction started, word spread around the surrounding community and attracted crowds of onlookers. Opening day, when we offered free lines, was like Christmas, Easter, and the Fourth of July, all rolled into one. For the first year we operated twenty-four hours a day and the place was always full. Things were going gangbusters and we were pretty proud of ourselves. At that time, FDIC insurance covered only the first $10,000 in any one bank account, so we had the fortunate problem of having to spread our cash among several banks. We were anticipating our first dividend when "it" happened. "It" was a combination of two things that occurred almost simultaneously. Bowling has always been a cyclical sport, with periodic ups and downs. In late 1963, it began one of the downs. At about the same time, the Civil Rights movement gathered steam, resulting in the "white" bowling alley, across town, being forced to open its doors to black people. And they went, even though the other alley had dated facilities and was not nearly as nice as ours.

Have you ever been in an empty bowling alley? It echoes. A dropped ball resonates like a cannon shot. With substantially reduced revenue, our equipment payments and rent quickly burned through our available cash. Sig and I scheduled a meeting with Brunswick and our landlord in Baltimore and handed them the keys. They were shocked. "But, you've always paid on time!" they said.

"That was then and now is now," we explained.

They reluctantly took over the facility and hired Sig as temporary manager. That arrangement lasted just a few months before the business was forced to bow to the inevitable. The equipment went into storage and the building became an industrial warehouse.

I don't know for sure, but I expect the people who beat us to Richmond suffered a similar fate.

Here's another example of what happens when you get a little ahead of yourself. Shortly after our move to Colorado, I had sold my interest in Tetra and the down payment was burning a hole in my pocket. I took the children to a local riding stable and met some of the wranglers. One day, one of them took me aside and said, "Ya know, Jay, we was thinkin' it shore would be nice to start a trail ridin' outfit." What they had in mind was a business taking tourists on day rides and camping trips in the mountains. What they also had in mind was finding someone to come up with the capital.

Boy, were they talking to the right sucker! Deep in most men's souls, certainly in mine, lies the image of themselves playing John Wayne and hollering, "Head 'em up, and move 'em out!" So, High Country Trails was born. After two years of steady losses, we sold the horses and closed up shop. Again, lack of enough revenue to cover expenses forced the demise.

What did we do wrong? For one thing, we did no market analysis whatsoever. The market at that time would not bear pricing sufficient to cover our costs. We had in our heads that we were going to run the business the "right way," using healthy, happy horses, serving top-quality food, and treating our guests like, well, guests. We weren't willing to cut corners to reduce our expenses. One of our competitors has remained successful in the business, because those things aren't important to him. He cuts corners. So goes the "dude" biz.

These misjudgments, combined with the relatively short riding season in Colorado, doomed the enterprise. But I had a ball while it lasted.

You might gather from the above examples that planning was not exactly my forte, and you'd be right. I've tended to go on gut feelings and I've been right, financially, much better than 50 percent of the time. That being said, I encourage you to learn from my experience. To increase your chances of success, I suggest you plan carefully, follow your plan, *modify it as necessary*, and track your progress.

Start or Buy?

When you decide to go into your own business, you basically have three options: you can start a new one, you can buy all or part of an existing one, or you can franchise.

Up to now, we've focused in this book on starting a business from scratch. I guess that's where the glory and the bragging rights are. There's nothing wrong, however, with acquiring a good business someone else started and then adding your own personal touch. The operative word, here, is "good." Over the years, as you might guess by now, I've done my share of horse trading, in the literal sense. I believe it's safe to say that a person generally doesn't sell a horse because he or she likes it so much. Someone posted some pretty funny (but with an element of truth) definitions of terms used in an ad about a horse for sale. Among them were "energetic" —horse runs away with a rider, "mature"—one foot in the grave, "spirited"—kicked his last owner into the next county, "green broke"—bucked off the last three people who tried to ride him, and so on. The same goes for small businesses. A business isn't usually put on the block because things are going perfectly and the owner is making too much money. There are exceptions, of course. My $75,000 investment in Tetra provided me with an increasing standard of living for fourteen years, plus a profit of almost 700 percent when I sold it.

Before and after Tetra, however, I've probably answered over one hundred want ads under "Businesses for Sale," chased down other leads, and talked to a lot of eager sellers. Some looked promising on the surface, but with a bit of digging, the skunk in the woodpile emerged. The lesson here is, do your homework.

Many of the techniques we'll discuss in the chapters on selling apply to buying, as well. Buying, whether it's a business or anything else, is selling in reverse. Other than a casual purchase in a store, you're often selling the seller on a lower price, better terms, additional features, etc. Perhaps the word "negotiating" better describes both sides of the process.

Buying an existing business

When you are considering a business to buy, before you ever get to the negotiating stage, you need to do what the big boys call "due diligence." This is really not an appropriate task for amateurs. Both the seller and the business broker, if one is involved, want only one thing: *your money*, and they will do almost anything to get it. The terms "lie, cheat, and steal" may be a little strong in this situation, but not by a whole lot. Unless you are *very* familiar with the industry and the particular business, you will need all the help you can get. This might include, in addition to a good lawyer and accountant, someone who *is* familiar with at least the type of business under consideration. Can you accurately analyze a balance sheet, a cash-flow statement, a profit and loss (P&L) statement? Who prepared these reports? Do you know the difference between audited, reviewed, and internally-prepared statements? Will you be buying the whole business or just the assets? Why is the owner selling? Will he or she base part or the entire purchase price on future performance? Will he/she finance all or part of the purchase price? Do you have to personally guarantee the balance? Is the property included in the sale, or can you assume the lease? Will the seller stay on for a period to help you get started? If so, how will he/she be compensated? What is the company's competitive position in its industry? What will be the future demand for its product or service? It's a lot to consider.

But we've only scratched the surface. You'll need to find competent help to come up with other questions and to help you find the answers.

Depending on the industry, a fair purchase price for a going business might range from five to ten times *net* annual earnings. That is after salaries (including the owner'(s), if active) but before taxes. That would mean that you should earn back your purchase price (again, before taxes) in five to ten years. If you were able to increase earnings, you'd earn your money back sooner.

Buying part of a going business, with or without an agreement or option to acquire the rest, could work, given the right mix of personalities. In this case, though, "Aim for the best, but anticipate the worst." The combination of a presumably older owner who is experienced in the business with a presumably younger one who can interject new energy and new ideas could be dynamite, in both senses of the word.

If you are considering this option, take note of the caveats in the sections dealing with partners, franchises, and family businesses. Structure your agreement *very* carefully. Make sure to cover duties and responsibilities, financial contributions and benefits, time and other commitments, dispute resolutions, and, worst-case, dissolution procedures.

My experience with this situation at Tetra was both good and bad. As the new kid, I had much to learn and had a good teacher. The "teacher," however, was less-than-tolerant of new-fangled ideas. An example was, believe it or not, the advantages of multi-page invoice and other form sets, as compared to good old-fashioned carbon paper. I can imagine the uproar had the issue of computer purchase come up in 1965! Also, as my percentage of ownership grew and his diminished, he spent less and less time and effort making the business grow. To be fair to him, why should he have? The price, as well as his salary, was fixed. The good news here was that as he gave up responsibility for various tasks, I had to step in and do them. It was a case of "learn or die." I chose to learn.

Probably the best situation is one in which you have the opportunity to acquire all or part of a business you've been working in right along. Gary Bennett, the husband of one of my riding buddies, was able to do this with a printing business for which he had been working since he was fifteen. He advanced from pushing a broom to being the owner's right-hand man. When the owner decided to retire, who better to take over? Gary's job titles, over the years, had included delivery driver and sales manager.

The owner had two daughters, one of whom worked in the business. Neither, however, expressed an interest in running it when the time came. By the time the owner wanted to retire, the two knew each other well enough that Gary had no problem financing the purchase on mutually acceptable terms.

Connie and Jim's purchase of Tetra from me was another example of a natural purchase opportunity. With the exception of sales, they'd been pretty much running the business for several years, and the transition was a no-brainer.

The next best thing to buying the company where you've worked, perhaps, would be buying a competitor's. While this might not endear you to your present employer, you'd have the advantage of already being familiar with both the industry and, to some extent, with both your current company's and the other company's strengths and weaknesses.

Meet your new partner—the franchise route

What about a franchise? Many early franchisees of national "name" products or services, such as McDonald's, Kinko's, and Midas, have done extremely well. Reports of others have not been so rosy. An article some time ago on Subway sandwich franchises described them as putting in big dollars, plus killer hours, for less take-home money than they could be making had they stayed with their previous jobs.

The franchiser will tout the advantages: a name that's become a household word, a ready-made product or service, professional assistance in site selection, construction and/or interior arrangement, management and employee training, etc. Remember, though, all these things come at a price. You will have, in effect, a senior partner. This "partner" may get paid before you do in the form of an annual franchise fee, a gross (not net) percentage of sales, and profits on company-mandated supply and/or inventory purchases. Your partner may also want to dictate pretty much how "your" business is run, with little or no input from you.

If you are considering a franchise, *learn, learn, learn* before you sign anything or put down any money. Read everything you can get your hands on, both from the company and from other sources. Be sure to talk to other franchisees, preferably over a meal or drinks away from their businesses. Visit their sites unannounced and observe how they handle sales, customer relations, and employee issues. Talk with their employees if you get the chance.

Get your hands on all available financial information about the company itself and about the franchisees. Finally, make a decision on whether what you'll be getting warrants what you'll be paying.

Many years ago, at Tetra, we used a consultant who also was employed by an association of Chicago-area McDonald's operators. Some of the stories he told about company/store owner relationships were not pretty. Among the issues disputed were advertising, location of competing stores, and, of course, money.

Another option to consider

Thinking about turning your hobby into a business? As usual, this could be a good idea or a bad one. One of my Bancard customers was Caboose Hobbies in Denver, one of the largest model-train stores in the country. When I asked Duane Miller, the owner, if he had an elaborate train setup at his house, he said no, that trains were his business, not his hobby. What he did in his spare time was play the bagpipes in a pipe and drum band. He felt that playing with his product would interfere with making appropriate business decisions.

On the other hand, one of my friends and customers in Chicago runs a model-soldier business on the side. I would venture a guess that a main purpose of this activity is to be able to buy pieces for his own extensive collection at dealer prices.

Raising Funds—Money, Money, Money, Who's Got the Money?

Unless your brother-in-law is a venture capitalist, you're going to need financing from somewhere. Having done a bang-up job on your business plan (you have, haven't you?) you not only know how much money you will need to get started (more than you thought, right?) but you also are prepared to go out and get it. What! You're not?

Okay, as you've figured out, money doesn't grow on trees. Where it grows is in the pockets of people who have been smart or lucky enough to acquire it. And these people, or banks, or other potential lenders, are generally concerned with only two things: (1.) How much can I make on my money? and (2.) I don't want to take any more risk with it than I have to. Banks, unlike entrepreneurs, don't intentionally take *any* risks.

Your job, therefore, is to locate these people and satisfy them on items (1) and (2) above. This is not easy.

Step 1 is to determine how much you and any partners can contribute. This is one of the first questions outside investors will ask. If you are hesitant to risk your hard-earned bread, it's a big red flag to them. The next step is to identify people who might want either to invest in your company or to lend you money.

Taking on investors could be an attractive idea for a number of reasons. Often they can take part in your business, perhaps as board members, (with or without pay) and offer sage advice. Also, you probably won't have to pay them back at any specific time; they will reap their reward when you do, when the business succeeds.

Places to look for investors are in family, friends, well-off people who might have an interest in your particular industry, and, of course, venture capitalists. Note that these last are also called "vulture capitalists." They have a habit of wanting their pound of flesh, and they use their own scale.

Here are some reasons not to take on investors:

1. If your business really takes off, you will be sharing a good part of the wealth.
2. The investors could very well feel, with some justification, that they should have a voice in the company's operation. This could limit your control.
3. There are various state and federal laws covering the sale of stock and you'll want legal advice to make sure you don't run afoul of any of them.
4. And, finally, should you and your investor(s) have a falling out along the way (just as when you take on partners), you may have a hard time resolving the matter to everyone's satisfaction.

The art of borrowing money

Another way to raise capital is to borrow it. The local bank is an obvious place to look. People often say that banks lend money only if you don't need it. This may be a slight exaggeration. Recently, a banker in rural Tennessee offered to lend us money if we would put an equal amount in a certificate of deposit in his bank. Give me a break! Bankers do, however, need to be really careful with their depositors' funds, and they are governed by a myriad of federal, state, and local laws.

The first thing your banker is concerned with is how and when the loan will be repaid. No matter what a good guy you are or how much interest you are willing to pay, it's not the banker's money and he or she will have a really bad day if you default on your loan. Here is where your well-written business plan comes in. If your plan makes sense and indicates a reasonable scenario for success and repayment of the loan, then the banker will be much more inclined to advance you some funds. Be aware that a bank, in order to protect its depositors and comply with banking regulations, will insist on collateral for any funds it advances. Most banks prefer real property as collateral. Calculate how much equity you have in your house. Compare this to the amount of money you think you will need to borrow. If you're planning to take out a mortgage to buy the location of your business, can you increase the amount of the mortgage and add to your start-up capital?

Another possible source you might consider is the Small Business Administration (SBA). The SBA doesn't actually lend money. What it will do is guarantee a loan from a bank, usually at a very favorable rate. You deal through a designated middleman, who, for a fee, will guide you through the considerable red tape involved in the process. This fee is paid directly from the loan proceeds. SBA-guaranteed loans are for a specified period of time. Obviously, you're in trouble if you don't make the payments. It'll also cost you penalty fees if you want to pay the loan off *ahead of time*, if, for example, you want to sell the business. We incurred a substantial penalty when we paid off the SBA loan on Bancard's building prior to the sale of the business. Also, bear in mind that an SBA loan can complicate the departure of any of the partners, since each of you will be guaranteeing the loan. You'll have to weigh the advantages of an SBA loan against the restrictions involved.

You might also consider borrowing money from the people you originally planned on taking on as investors. While they might not want to take a chance counting on the success of your business, they may be more inclined to lend you money at a specified rate of interest for a specified term. This way they will (at least theoretically) be paid even if you starve. Unless they are pretty unsophisticated, they will give your business plan pretty much the same once- and twice-over that a bank would.

Location—Where, Oh, Where, Will My Little Business Grow?

The real estate people say that only three things matter: location, location, location. Your "housing" needs will vary considerably and will depend, to a great extent, on the type of product or service you plan to offer. If you will be consulting, you can probably get by with a small office. If you plan to make it big producing toxic chemicals, you'll need an entirely different setup.

A home office? An executive suite? A loft? A small industrial building? A store? These are all potential options. How close do you need to be to your suppliers? To your customers? What about zoning? Will your company's facilities need to be fancy or just homey? You need to plan for growth right from the start. Moving is expensive and not just in the obvious ways. Reprinting stationery, getting new phone numbers, rewiring, inconveniencing your employees, updating customers and other contact information—all of these things can cost plenty in time and money. You don't want to go overboard and spend all your initial capital on rent, but give some thought, when you select your first location, to your needs for the future.

More and more people are finding they can start businesses and run them for some time out of their house or apartment. A big advantage to this, besides saving on rent, is the convenience of being able to get up from the breakfast table and get right to work. Disadvantages include distractions from family, possible objections from neighbors, and the local zoning regulations.

Another possible disadvantage might be kids screaming or dogs barking when you're on the phone with an important customer.

If you do decide to work at home, it is important to have a separate space or, preferably, a separate room that serves as your office. Make sure your spouse and your children know that when you're at work, *you're at work*, and you're not to be disturbed. Have a separate phone line that will be answered in a businesslike manner and will not be monopolized by other family members or answered inappropriately. You may want to list that number in the Yellow Pages.

The Internal Revenue Service allows a deduction for space that is used *solely* for business. Think twice about taking this deduction, however. The rules are complex and having taken the deduction may complicate tax reporting on the eventual sale of your house. Further, it's rumored that the appearance of this deduction on a return increases the chance of receiving an audit.

Some businesses can make do with a virtual office—a service that can provide answering services, a mail address, and, perhaps, meeting facilities.

Legal Matters—Have you heard the one about the lawyer and...?

Before we get into this, I need to make the usual disclaimer. I am not giving legal or financial advice here. The material that follows, while I believe it to be valid, is my opinion only. Before you act on anything I say, I suggest you contact a qualified legal and/or accounting professional.

Having said that, I'll skip the lawyer jokes and get right to business. Abraham Lincoln said, "A man who is his own lawyer has a fool for a client." For the most part, I agree. A *good* lawyer, who truly has your interest at heart, is worth what he or she charges. Finding the right one, however, is not always easy. Lawyers, like people in most professions, come in all flavors:

excellent, good, mediocre, really bad. You probably don't want to pick one out of the Yellow Pages, now that attorneys can advertise. I'd suggest you ask for recommendations from people you know who have employed lawyers *for business issues.*

Most good attorneys should welcome a no-charge interview, with a general discussion of what you want a lawyer to do for you. Don't be afraid to ask about fees and charges. I have generally found it wise to utilize the best lawyer I could afford, and that probably means taking on one of the larger law firms. While the hourly rates offered by a one- or two-person firm may sound attractive, there are good reasons to go with a larger firm. Business law is complex and no one person can be an expert on all of its ramifications. Attorneys in larger firms generally specialize in one or more topics and won't need to be brought up to speed, when necessary, on an arcane matter. The person you normally deal with may want to bring another, better-qualified partner or associate in on particular matters. The resources of a larger firm will allow your lawyer to draw on the expertise of the entire firm.

Further, much of the "scut work" can be done by clericals or paralegals, and these individuals should bill at lower rates. One of the larger Denver firms we used announced that they will no longer bill for "soft costs": copying, faxes, postage, telephone, etc. They bill plenty for time spent, however.

Be certain that you and your attorney have charted a path that will keep you clear of legal minefields. Your attorney should ensure that you remain in compliance with applicable laws and regulations: local, state, and federal.

What happens when you *don't* get the best legal advice? I was told by the seller of Tetra, who happened to be a lawyer (non-practicing, at the time), that although we shipped a number of orders to customers in California, we had no liability for sales taxes to the State of California because we had no office in that state.

One day, about a year after said seller had departed to cash the check for the final installment on the deal, I arrived a little late that morning to find a stranger sitting in my office, in my chair. Our offices at the time had no waiting room. The gentleman identified himself as an Illinois representative of the California Department of Equalization, which is the agency concerned with collecting sales and use tax for the State of California. He informed me that, contrary to my ex-partner's advice, we indeed did owe taxes to California. Unless we could collect these taxes from the respective buyers, we would have to pay them ourselves, along with penalties, for sales in California during a period of up to three years previously. We began a frantic search for old invoices.

I lucked out in two respects: First, a large portion of the sales had been to the Los Angeles County Hospitals, who had dutifully paid their portion of the taxes. Second, California took pity on us and settled for taxes and penalties on the balance for just a one-year period.

It was an expensive wakeup call, though, and I have since been careful to comply with the tax laws of the various states in which we have done business. I have also been a little more careful in selecting my advisors.

Improperly accounting for withheld federal and state payroll taxes has tripped up many a budding businessperson. You will be required to withhold taxes from yourself and from your employees, to match their Social Security contributions, to calculate unemployment contributions, and to pay these in a timely manner to the various agencies. Once accrued, this is no longer your money. You need to safeguard it until it is paid and you can't use it for other business purposes. Failure to handle these funds properly is one obligation from which corporate or LLC status will not shield you. You will be held personally liable for any payments due, plus penalties and interest. You will also need to make unemployment and workmen's compensation fund payments. We'll have more on this when we discuss accounting. Check both the IRS website and your state's website for helpful information.

What form should your business take?

You will need to decide on a form for your business. These are your choices: Sole Proprietor, Partnership, Regular Corporation (C Corp), S Corporation (S Corp), and Limited Liability Company (LLC). Some states have added a few more names, but the above are the most common.

I'll repeat the warning I gave at the beginning of this section and ask that you do not treat the following as legal or accounting advice. Although I believe it to be accurate, it is only my opinion.

A **sole proprietorship** is just what it says—you are the business. You report income from it on Schedule C of your individual income tax return and you are *personally liable* for the actions, omissions, and debts of the company. A **partnership** is similar to a sole proprietorship, but it involves two or more people. Unless otherwise specified in the partnership agreement, the *consent of all partners* is required for any company actions. In both forms, the owner or owners pay taxes on all earnings, whether or not the earnings are distributed. Also, owners usually can deduct any losses against other income.

I suggest you *do not use* either of the above forms. Both involve unlimited personal liability. Should your business get involved in a legal action, your personal assets would be at risk. Additionally, in a partnership (other than a limited partnership) each partner is *responsible for and liable for the actions and business obligations of all other partners.*

A **standard corporation** ("C Corp.") pays taxes on its earnings and accrues losses against future profits. Dividends declared are taxable to the various shareholders. Other than for certain items, such as employment taxes withheld but not paid, shareholders are *not personally liable* for the corporation's actions and debts. The federal government has recently reduced taxes on dividends. However, the corporation still pays taxes on profits and the shareholders are taxed again, at the reduced rate, for any dividends received. This form of business is probably most applicable when the company needs to retain a large portion of its earnings to finance fixed assets or inventory, since the company will probably pay taxes at a lower rate than an individual owner.

S Corps and LLC's provide the liability protection of a corporation but are taxed like a sole proprietorship or partnership, although an LLC can elect to be taxed like a C Corp. There are restrictions on the number and type of shareholders in an S Corp. An LLC provides greater flexibility in this regard. Under certain circumstances, a business may change its form later on.

We have only skimmed the surface of this topic. Discuss it with your lawyer and your accountant, and be certain you agree on the best form for you and your business.

A few more legal matters I'd like to discuss with you.

Try to have a clear understanding with your attorney of how you will be billed. On complex matters, try to get an estimate of the maximum cost involved. Especially if you are using a small firm, ask questions and satisfy yourself that the lawyer has a reasonable grasp of the subject matter involved. You don't want to pay a lot of money to have your lawyer learn on the job. Don't hesitate to inform him or her that you will be consulting another lawyer, as appropriate, should matters arise that are outside his or her areas of expertise.

Finally, take a lesson from one who has been there and don't spend of lot of money "for the principle of the thing." During the process of buying our first computer at Tetra, I felt the original vendors had misrepresented their ability to produce what was specified. After the third "Well, what did you expect?" following installation of the equipment, I told them to take it back and ignored the invoice. They sued and, after many depositions, dropped the suit "on the courthouse steps." Our legal bills came to around $10,000, and that was back in 1970 when $10,000 was a lot of money. Our lawyers said that we could have settled along the way for less. When push comes to shove, consider the value of your time and the cost of proving that you are right. Sometimes, it pays to say, "Oh, well," and settle.

Human Resources—To Be a Better Boss Than My Boss

Human Resources is much more than hiring, firing, and keeping records.

An excellent work force doesn't "just happen." It is, as you'll remember, one leg of the Milking Stool. Ask any successful business owner what the company's most important asset is and I'd bet the answer would be, "Our people."

I got an important lesson in management many years ago. I was in college and the Korean War was on. We had the choice of either burying our heads and being drafted after college or doing something about it. I chose to take matters into my own hands and joined the Reserve Officers Training Corps.

After college, as a new second lieutenant in an Air Force squadron in Germany, one of my assignments was supervising the Air Police detachment. Some months later, as one of my troops was leaving for "Stateside" and discharge, he shook my hand and said, "Lieutenant, I hope we meet up sometime in the States...." I felt pretty good about this compliment to my newly learned management style, until I heard his next words, "so I can shove that gold bar up your ____." Obviously, I still had a way to go in perfecting my supervisory skills.

The "in-way" to manage seems to change with the season. "Quality Circles," "Empowerment," "Team," "Customer-Oriented," "TQM." There seems to be no end to the buzzwords. Unless you envision remaining a one-person business, however, you need to start somewhere. Again, there are stacks of books on the subject of management, and reading one or two probably won't do you any harm. Give some thought, though, to the first book on management. "Do unto others," and you know the rest. Sounds simple? It's easy to say. It's another thing to do.

I believe that management or, better, leadership, bears a close resemblance to salesmanship. Just as you can sell a product or service, you can "sell" an idea to a coworker or employee. "Because I said so," may work with your children (or it may not), but it doesn't work too well with employees or coworkers. You need to have a buy-in from your employees or their hearts won't be in it. When we were kids, we sang a version of a Ledbetter song. We changed the lyrics a bit:

This land is my land,/It isn't your land.
You'd better get off,/Or I'll blow your head off.
I've got a shotgun,/And you ain't got one.
This land is mine and mine alone.

It may, indeed, be your company, but you probably need other people to help make it work well. Think a minute, why do *you* do what you do? Because you feel that doing these things will somehow benefit you. This applies to the people you work with also. It's important for them to see how taking an action will benefit them. Psychologists call this "protracted self-interest."

Take my present situation. I am presently in a position to contribute a fair amount of both money and time to non-profit organizations. Most of these organizations are animal-related. Why donate time and money? Is it for the animals? Sure, but this may not be the principal reason. I'm getting something out of it, too. You and I get numerous phone calls and letters for causes that may or may not be worth donating to. Do we contribute? That depends on how we relate to the pitch. How much do we contribute? Five bucks? Ten? Why do we do this? Because it makes us feel good. Do we know, however, that all our money is going to the worthy cause? Does it matter to us? Mostly we write the check and forget it.

Now imagine if the Executive Director and Development Director of an organization responded to your donation with presents for your horse, flowers for your spouse, and an invitation to lunch? Do you suppose that'd make you feel pretty good about your gift, and favorably inclined toward supporting the organization in the future? It sure did for us. Have we made further contributions to that organization? Take a guess. Everyone gets something out of it. The organization gets the money it needs. I get the positive feeling that people appreciate my contribution, and my horses get carrots. Protracted self-interest in action.

Another principle I believe in is leading by example. Where do you suppose the great military leaders of the past, from Alexander to Sherman to Patton, were, during the major battles? Safe back at headquarters? Nope! They had been taught, or knew instinctively, that you LEAD BY EXAMPLE. Soldiers are inspired to do what they have to do when they see their leaders LEADING.

I don't think management (again, I prefer "LEADership") is a big mystery. What people want to know is, "What's in it for *me*?" They've got bills to pay and (hopefully) they take pride in doing a good job. Most everyone wants to feel they are contributing toward a common goal. The current term "stakeholder" implies giving them "a piece of the action."

How do you "give 'em a piece of the action"?

You can accomplish this in a number of ways. One way is to give or sell your employees part of the company. A method for doing this is through an Employee Share Ownership Trust (ESOT). ESOTs were all the rage a few years ago. Through an ESOT you can give your employees ownership benefits while retaining voting control for yourself. You can also, depending on your company's value at the time, derive substantial tax benefits. An ESOT arrangement is probably pretty far down the pike for you. It's not something you need to concern yourself with at the outset of the business. Sometimes an ESOT fails to accomplish its intended purpose. Take the case of United Airlines. Prior to the current bankruptcy situation, the "owner-employees" seemed to have no compunction about demanding the highest wage scale in the industry or threatening to strike against "their" company.

Another way to give 'em a piece is to sell or give your employees (or at least the key ones) actual partial ownership of the company. Be careful of this one also. Things change, people change. One day you turn around and people you thought you knew are telling you how it is. What you felt was an act of generosity and the right thing to do can come up to bite you, big time. How big? Well, let's just say that your author learned this lesson to the tune of several million dollars. And there was a whole line of people waiting to tell me, "We told you so!" More on this particular incident later.

How, then, do you "give 'em a piece of the action" without stepping in something messy and malodorous down the line? Consider this: "Ownership" can take many forms. Just making your employees aware of "the big picture" and how they fit in can be very effective. Keeping employees in the dark is counterproductive. Too many managers try to boost their own egos on the theory that "I know something and you don't, which makes me more important than you." This is a very good way to take away people's motivation. Dilbert's boss, the man with the pointy-hair and the bad attitude, is a very good illustration of this point.

Probably the first step in this process is to find out what your people want, individually and collectively. Forget the stick—what would be an effective carrot? This question is not as easy as it appears. Do they want money? Probably. Recognition? Almost certainly. Good working conditions? Yeah, but who defines what "good" means? The best way to find out what they want is to ask and *keep asking*. "What would you like to get out of this job, this company?" Once you feel you have the answer(s), you need to align the employee's goals and benefits with the company's goals. *This is a key issue*. A happy ship is a productive one. It's also important for everyone to know where he or she really fits in the corporate structure.

At Bancard, we had an organizational chart that looked a little different from others you may have seen. Rather than the traditional pyramid, with the CEO at the top and the LPDs (Lowly Damn Peasants) at the bottom, ours was a circle. At the center, in big letters, it read: THE CUSTOMER! After all, didn't the customers give all of us orders, in both senses of the word? You bet! And who was on the next ring? The people who took orders (in both senses of the word) from the customers:

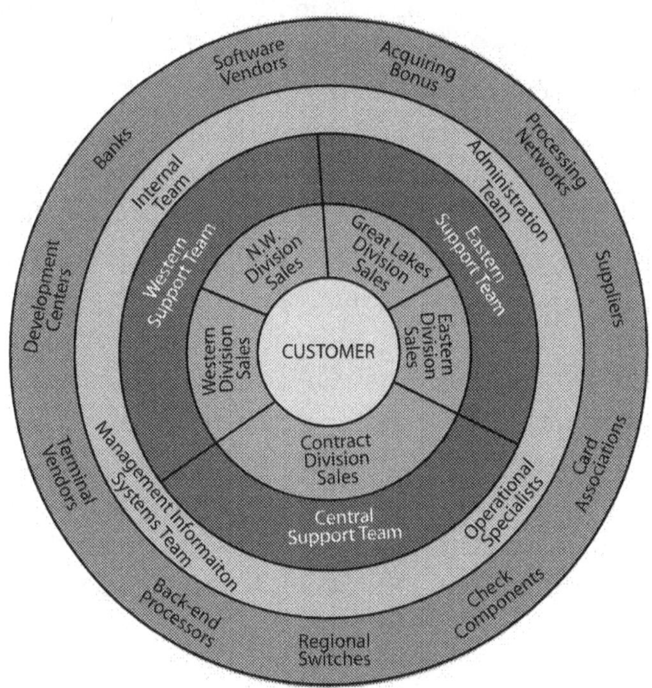

the SALESPEOPLE. And next? The people who supported the sales people as well as the customers: THE FIRST-LEVEL SUPPORT TEAMS.

And, who was relegated to the outside? Everybody else, from the sanitation engineers to the CEO. Were they less important to the company? The people in the outer rings, including me, supported the people who supported the people who supported the people at the center of our business: THE CUSTOMERS.

Did we mean what we said? Did we really see our company that way? You bet your bippy! And it worked.

To sum up, if you are the leader, then **LEAD!** Lead from the front and "Do unto others...."

A few words about Human Resources

We could have treated Human Resources separately from management, but in a small company, they go hand-in-hand. The boss, the leader, will probably do most of the hiring and, when necessary, the firing. Obviously, the Golden Rule applies here also. From a financial, an ethical and, increasingly, a legal standpoint, you will want to treat your employees fairly.

Having a comprehensive, well-written personnel manual is a good start. I've included a sample in the Appendix. It is only a sample. Please feel free to adapt it to your own requirements, but you will need to revise your manual from time to time, as things change. You also can purchase a sample or pay, as we did, to have one custom written for your company. You might want to discuss your manual with your attorney or someone familiar with personnel matters and labor law in your state. Be certain to provide a copy of the original, as well as subsequent revisions, to each employee and new hire. Have them sign a receipt, and make certain to retain a copy of their signed acknowledgment in their personnel file. This can really help you in the event of a dispute later on.

Let's talk about hiring. It is pretty well accepted these days by enlightened employers that you want the best-qualified person for the job, be that person a he or a she, white, black, brown, or green. You not only need to believe this yourself, but you need to make sure *all your people believe this*, as well. Many companies find themselves in a big pile of something nasty because one or more of their managers or workers failed to learn this valuable lesson. Note, we said best *qualified* person. Larger companies can give lip service to the idea of training the untrainable, of going to extremes to appear politically correct. You probably can't, at least at first. One good place, though, to look for really good, dedicated workers is among the disabled. People who lack the use of one or more bodily functions often make up for that loss by developing extra skill in other areas.

Before you even start the hiring process, write down a clear, complete job description of the position(s) to be filled. Include, at minimum, duties, hours, pay, incentives, benefits, supervisor, and opportunities for advancement. It is best if you can involve someone who is performing or has performed this job in the hiring process.

Next, bone up on federal, local, and state regulations on the subject of hiring. These are subject to change, so make sure to refer to the appropriate agencies and their websites or to an attorney who is familiar with this aspect of the law. These regulations cover everything from the wording of your ads to what you can and can't do, say, and ask in an interview.

Be sure to emphasize, both verbally and in writing, that *employment is for an indefinite period* and may be terminated by the company for any reason. This will not relieve you of your responsibility to keep accurate employee records and document the reasons for your actions, but it can help you win a dispute after an involuntary termination.

We experimented with various psychometric testing products, with mixed results. The tests might have prevented our wasting time with obvious losers. I have my doubts, however, that they were effective in selecting the best candidates.

When you think of hiring, give considerable thought to firing. Firing is an unpleasant but inevitable consequence. We would like to hire only brilliant, competent, loyal employees who will work their heads off and stay forever. However, termination, downsizing, or whatever the current term is, is bound to happen.

We were fortunate, for the most part, at Bancard. We were able keep this problem to a minimum. As we grew we developed a corporate culture that enabled us to more accurately select who fit our collective mold and who would be less likely to work out. Early on, when we still had just a few employees, I somehow developed the idea that it was unfair to terminate people at work. I felt that it would be better to take them to lunch, drop the bad news on them there, and offer to pack up their things if they didn't want to return to the office. Pretty soon it was hard to find anyone who wanted to go to lunch with me. So I stopped doing this.

Along the way, without a whole lot of input from management, a team concept grew. Members of the various departments began to bond, to support each other, and to weed out on their own folks who couldn't or wouldn't do their share. As the company grew larger and more sophisticated, we reinforced this concept with team bonuses. In the last year or so prior to the sale of the business, we froze all salaries and hourly wages. With the exception of company officers and of the sales force, who worked on straight commission and were able to control their own earnings, everyone in the company received a monthly bonus. This bonus was based partly on a percentage of the net profit for the month and partly on the teams' achievement of pre-specified goals. For the longer-term employees, the bonus often exceeded their salaries or wages.

This intensified the intra-team discipline. The team itself could make life so unpleasant for people not pulling their weight that they often quit of their own accord.

As a manager, you will need to monitor this type of activity, so that the company doesn't run afoul of employment and civil rights regulations.

One glaring exception to our success in managing human resources issues was the case of our first senior management hire. This individual was a former customer who had disposed of his company, gone through a divorce, and moved from the mountains of Colorado to the Denver area. He had run all phases of a successful property-management company. My primary interest was sales and marketing, not operations. So I jumped at the chance to hire him when he became available. By this time, our company was growing rapidly and things were beginning to slip through the cracks. Computers were just coming into general use, and this person, whom we will call "Ralph," had taught himself on the use of computers. His knowledge and skill with computers was far beyond mine.

Ralph took to his new job with a vengeance. Among other things, he shepherded us past the computer system we were using, a 64-byte CPM system. "What's that?" you ask. It was the operating system that predated DOS and Windows, way back in the pre-historic age of computers. He brought us into the world of Microsoft and PCs. He also implemented a database and upgraded our accounting system. We could now handle accounting internally, instead of relying on an outside bookkeeper. Ralph became, in my eyes, so integral to the company's future that I almost forced him to "buy," for the token sum of $5,000, shares amounting to a 15 percent interest in the company. I also gave him an option to buy another 5 percent in a two-year period for another $5,000. On top of that, he had a very lucrative employment contract. As if that weren't enough, I personally lent him the down payment to purchase a house in Boulder so that he would no longer have to commute from Denver.

Unfortunately, as the company continued to grow, as our work force approached 150 people, Ralph did not keep pace. One day, two of our mid-level supervisors asked me to dinner. The gist of the dinner conversation was that either Ralph had to go or they would leave. They said that most of the other managers would also leave. I had noticed Ralph occasionally acting inappropriately with employees and had discussed it with him. I felt that he was making an effort to deal with this problem. Obviously, I wasn't clear on how bad things were.

Horrified, I met with my other partner, our West Coast Regional Sales Manager, who had been given an identical share-purchase arrangement. After talking again with the supervisors and with our attorney, we met with Ralph, told him he was being terminated, and gave him thirty days' salary in lieu of the notice called for in his contract.

This left us with the problem of how to deal with his share ownership and the further problem of an action he brought for unjust termination. For reasons I can't go into here, we eventually settled the suit for about $300,000 and managed to purchase his shares back for around half a million. You win some and you lose some, and we sure lost that one.

Looking back, I'm not certain how it could have been handled differently. There was no way we could have kept Ralph on. Letting him work out his thirty days' notice period would have caused chaos for the company.

I have included this lengthy confession just to make you aware of the types of landmines that can lie on the road of hiring and personnel management.

HR and salespeople: Keep hands and feet away from the cage at all times

Our other significant "downsizing" problems generally involved salespeople. We will go into this further when we discuss sales and sales management. Salespeople are funny folks. They don't always view life as everyone else does. A salesperson is always searching for something that's in great demand, which he/she can give away for nothing, and that pays a big commission. Salespeople are experts in trying to beat the system. I feel certain that if they would expend the same amount of time and effort on selling as they do on system-beating, they would make a lot more money.

Make sure you carefully structure contract arrangements with your sales force, *in writing.* State exactly what you expect each of them to do and how and when they will be compensated for their labors. Also, make sure to spell out what will happen if they *don't* perform and *when* it will happen.

In my experience, two groups of salespeople will cause you the most personnel problems: the sub-par people and—the superstars. Let's deal with the poor performers first. The way to deal with these folks is to identify them quickly and get rid of them equally quickly. The 80/20 rule applies here. Just as your top 20 percent will produce 80 percent of the business, more or less, the bottom 20 percent will cause 80 percent of the grief. Grief may include whining, complaining, lying, and even outright dishonesty. We had one salesperson who established a bank account for himself as Bancard and cashed checks from his customers made out to the company. Someone or something solved the problem before we did, as he managed to run his car into a tree at high speed and do away with himself.

Left to continue rotting, these apples can contaminate a good part of the organization. Remember, you're not running a social service organization. You're running a business. Let your competitors have the pleasure of these folks' company.

Often when salespeople leave they intimate or threaten that all their accounts will leave too. Don't you believe it! If you've done any kind of job on customer service, the majority of *your* (not the salesperson's) customers will not inconvenience themselves by switching. A well-written non-compete agreement will discourage a departing salesperson from trying to steal your customers, but excellent customer service is much better insurance.

Now, let's talk about our other group of problem children: the super producers. We're not speaking about the top 20 percent, just the two or three real superstars. These people are driven to excel and to make money. Nothing or nobody had better get in their way. To them, the sun rises and sets, first on themselves and, second, on THEIR customers. If you handle them right, they can be among your best assets. However, they can play hell with your support troops. You, as the business owner, will need to try to satisfy both sides. You might consider linking all or part of the support folks' bonuses to the salesperson's production. This could go a long way toward fostering cooperation and reducing friction. We implemented this at Bancard. The number of accounts signed by the sales division they supported determined part of our teams' bonuses. This caused them to be more tolerant of the various salespeople's eccentricities.

A few final thoughts on management and HR

One of the taxes you will pay is an item called Unemployment Benefits. This is a joint program of the federal government and the various states. The amount you pay starts off relatively high and can increase or decrease depending on how many of your ex-employees file successful claims. If you fire someone, unless you can prove cause—such as a work-related felony or misdemeanor—he/she will generally be awarded unemployment benefits. If an employee quits, it is up to him/her to prove duress. Unfortunately for you, the bureaucrats employed in this system tend to take the employee's side in any dispute. Nevertheless, in order to keep your rate as low as possible, it will pay you to dispute any claim where you have a leg to stand on.

I need to end this section by putting on my clerical garb again and doing a little more preaching. We've touched on the subject of business ethics and will revisit it later in the book. But I want to take a few moments to discuss business ethics as they apply to personnel management. Let's put it this way: **Good ethics is good business.** It just makes sense that, if you treat people right, chances are they'll reciprocate. In one of the Dr. Seuss books I used to read to my children, Horton the Elephant would say, "I meant what I said and I said what I meant. An elephant's truthful one hundred percent." I don't want to undercut the importance of having written, signed records of important understandings. However, if people know that, "Your word is your bond," it will save a lot of time.

If your people see you dipping your hand in the cash register, what're they going to think? Something like, "If the boss does it, it should be okay for me to do it." If you are less than honest with a customer or a vendor, your employees will learn from that example. What's more, if you get caught, one of your employees could get called to testify against you in a court of law.

Going back to the subject of negotiating for a minute, my advice is, "Bargain hard, but bargain fair." If your employees see you putting the squeeze on people all the time, then they'll figure it's okay to do the same, even against you. We had a sales manager at Tetra who had no compunction about lying to a vendor or a prospective vendor. He would rattle off fictitious low competitive pricing without a moment's hesitation. It always made me squirm, and I wonder how many of his customers were doing the same to him.

It is tempting to go for the last chip on the table, but what happens the next time you meet the same people at another table? Will they remember you as a good guy to do business with or as a shark?

Your employees' actions reflect on you, as well. One of our salespeople at Tetra fancied himself a ladies' man. He felt he was

God's gift to every female nurse and technician in each hospital he called on.

I can remember sitting with him in a bar after work one day and hearing him say, "I bet I can do that woman."

My response was, "Her husband's probably in your hometown, saying the same thing about your wife."

It didn't help matters when we later got a call from a nursing supervisor at one of the hospitals. She "suggested" we speak to young Romeo and ask him to cool it. These days, the call might well have been from the hospital's lawyer.

I lost touch with him after we left Chicago, so I don't know the end of that story. I do know, however, about one of our salespeople at Bancard who had a similar attitude. He ended up in divorce court, where I assume his wife was awarded half of the money he had made during his employment and as a result of the company's sale. This was tough on him, but even tougher on their three children.

Before I step out of the pulpit, I need to remind you of another phrase from the Bible: "As ye sow, so shall ye reap." It's important to consider at all times the example you are setting.

Operations—The Art of Building Mouse Traps

There are three ways to target a successful product or service, all of them akin to various water sports. The first two have to do with surfing.

- You can find a wave and ride it. (This is what we did with Bancard and the surge in credit card usage.)
- You can create your own wave. (Microsoft and Xerox are good examples of companies that followed this path.)
- Or, you can just jump into the pool and start swimming like hell. (This is what we did with Tetra, the medical supply company. We picked our products, improved them where we could, and just outsold and outpriced our competition.)

All three work.

A word about service. I attended a weeklong bankcard school given by the American Bankers Association. One of the speakers was Dee Hock, former CEO of Visa International. Mr. Hock is generally credited with much of Visa's early success. As a private citizen and a gentleman farmer, he could be much more candid and graphic than he could in his previous profession. During his talk, he defined "service" as "what the bull does to the cow." This was, for me, an epiphany. The key to competing with the banks was **service**. Getting out and selling would help also.

It is my experience that many companies and most banks "serve" their employees and customers the way Mr. Hock put it, which is why going to the bank, whether to make a deposit or to get a loan, is about as much fun as having a root canal. I believe that most CEOs today assume their companies provide good customer service. The message seems to get lost, however, between the head honcho and the worker bees. I think most of us, as consumers and customers, would tend to agree with this.

Bancard's secret weapon became—you guessed it—The Milking Stool. Our idea was to create a company that used the more commonly accepted definition of service. We treated our vendors well and they, in turn, gave us pretty good pricing and service. We treated our employees well so that they would treat our customers well. This system worked fine. To the day I left, we had a real person answering the phones. I often told Marnie she *was* the company to the people calling in. Each time I told her, she glowed.

Outside sales and service of bankcard processing was a brand new thing, so we had to write the book as we went along. As bankcard processing got more and more efficient, faster, and complex, we were forced to learn on the job.

The nice thing about our business, for both the company and the sales force, was that we sold the service once and, as long as we kept our customers happy, we got paid forever. This certainly provided the incentive to keep them happy.

Early on, you probably made a decision on your intended price point and where your product would fit on the quality scale. There's a market for Yugos, just as there is a market for Lexuses. The key here is value, both actual and perceived. If your customers feel they are getting value for their money, they will keep buying from you, and will tell their friends. If, in their minds, your product is shoddy, they will tell their friends that. "Planned obsolescence" can be good or bad, depending on whether you're buying or selling. Probably a good compromise here is to produce a product that works fine, gives good service, but then offer a model that is "newer!—better!"

Carrying the water analogy one step further, some business owners load themselves with weights (mistakes) and sink to the bottom. One of the primary purposes of this book is to help you avoid that fate. Others find the wave dying out, or stop swimming and just float. Unless they get moving again, sooner or later, they, too, will start to sink.

You will need to determine which seems appropriate for you. Find the wave, make your own, or start swimming.

As a general comment, just be sure you can produce your product or service at a price that will allow you to sell it competitively and in sufficient quantities, at a reasonable profit.

Accounting—A Bean Counter? Who? Me?

It's time for the disclaimer, again: The material that follows, while I believe it to be valid, does not constitute legal or financial advice. Prior to acting on it, I suggest you consult a qualified legal and/or financial professional.

Someone (probably an accountant) once said, "The language of business is numbers." Imagine a submarine without a periscope. Try to picture the Lone Ranger thundering across the prairie on the Great Horse Silver without a bridle. You've just imagined a company that doesn't keep a timely and accurate set of books.

Properly maintained books can tell you much more than just where the company's been. A carefully designed, consciously maintained balance sheet, profit and loss statement, and other reports derived from the same sources can show you what you're doing right and, perhaps more importantly, what you're doing wrong.

A careful review of the books can answer a number of important questions. Are we making progress or slipping backward? What are we doing right, and where are the holes in the dyke? What can we do best to plug these holes? Do we have too much cash on hand? This would not be likely, at least in the initial stages, but it is possible. Are we paying too much for raw material? For supplies? For labor?

A **Sales Analysis** can show you which of your sales efforts and/or salespeople are paying off and which need changes or "counseling." An **Aged Accounts Receivable Report** (if you have to sell on credit) will indicate which of your customers' accounts may need a little attention.

Unfortunately, many businesspeople have an insufficient knowledge of accounting. As a result they become all too dependent upon the "bookkeeper." Unless the boss has a working knowledge of bookkeeping/accounting, then the boss has no basis for evaluating the "bookkeeper's" competence and honesty. Yes, I did say honesty. Where there's cash, there's temptation. Good ol' Bill or Sadie might have problems you can't *imagine*, which might cause him or her to "borrow a little cash just for a while."

"Bill" and "Sadie" are fictitious names, of course, but Michelle Lee Stevens and Elaine Brewer are not. An article in the *Daily Camera* (Boulder, Colorado) issue of May 31, 2002, headlined, "Woman Accused of Stealing from Her Friend's Business," stated that Ms. Stevens was "suspected" of embezzling more than $90,000 from her best friend's business.

"I trusted Michele 100 percent," said Stephanie Moore, owner of Becoming Mothers Store. According to the story, Ms.

Stephens admitted to police that she had taken the money "to get by" as a single mother and had every intention to pay it back. I say, "Yeah, right." With friends like these, who needs enemies?

Here's another sad story from the Associated Press: Elaine Brewer, of Colorado Springs, Colorado, was sentenced to seven years in prison for stealing "more than $207,000" from the Cheyenne Mountain Zoo where she was the top financial officer. The zoo's president and chief executive was quoted as saying, "We trusted Elaine as a member of our team, and she badly betrayed that trust." I'll say! Note how the word "trust" appears in both quoted statements. I have a newspaper article telling similar stories of eight more people on Colorado's Front Range.

We had a bookkeeper at Bancard who initially seemed to be competent. As time went by, however, he developed some suspicious habits. For one, he was always weeks late in cashing his paycheck. Also, he hated to have anyone stand behind him and look over his shoulder at his work. Finally, he never left his desk without turning his computer off. After he left, we never could prove that he stole, but he sure left the books in a mess. It wasn't clear that he was doing anything dishonest. It became apparent, though, that he certainly had not been up to the job. When I interviewed his prospective replacement, I asked her if she was willing to tackle a real bag of worms. She was and soon had things running smoothly.

I'm not trying to scare you with these stories to imply that every bookkeeper is a potential criminal. Just make certain that when you hire someone for this job, you carefully check references and establish a strong set of controls. It's your money, and no one can do a better job of watching it than you can.

One more thing. I strongly suggest you *do not* delegate the job of signing the checks. Insist that each check presented for your signature be accompanied by the corresponding invoice or other supporting documentation. Question anything that seems unclear to you.

Choosing the right person to count the beans

My dictionary defines "bookkeeping" as "the theory and practice of keeping records of monetary transactions" and "accounting" as "the keeping and *auditing* [italics mine] of financial records." That would seem to say that if you just want someone to handle the books, use a bookkeeper. If you want your books kept and audited, you need an accountant. In practice, finding the right person is not quite that simple. Just as anyone can call himself a bookkeeper, so it is with the term "accountant." A certified public accountant (CPA), on the other hand, must have had a prescribed course of instruction and passed a rigorous examination. Which do you need? That depends on what you want done. Unless you're up on bookkeeping, you will probably want a competent accountant, at least to set up your books for the first time. You'll also want a competent accountant to review the books at least once a year, probably at tax time. Doing your own books may or may not be the best use of your time.

Many small businesses use an outside bookkeeper or bookkeeping service on a part-time basis to do most of the record-keeping. I will use the terms "bookkeeping" and "accounting" interchangeably in this book, just to avoid monotony.

As with any professional, you will want to shop around and satisfy yourself that your outside accountant/bookkeeper is the best you can afford. Check credentials and ask for references.

I used the term "audit" earlier. An audit involves a thorough examination of the books, including queries to suppliers and customers who have had financial transaction with the company. A review, on the other hand, is just that. The accountant reviews the company's books to make sure transactions have been reported correctly. The cost of a review should be much less than the cost of an audit. Unless you are planning to go public or have grown pretty big, you probably will need nothing more than a review. Even that may not be necessary during the first few years. You will, however, want to make certain your taxes are computed and paid correctly and on time.

Keeping the books was one of the first things I delegated, both at Tetra and at Bancard. I can do it if I have to, but I can make more money and have more fun doing other things. For the first several years at Bancard, I prepared the federal and state tax returns, myself. At first I did them by hand and later by computer, using tax-preparation software. During this time, I had become friends with a CPA by the name of Peggy Topel, who worked with a medium-sized accounting firm in Denver and did the books for a condominium association I oversaw for a time. When she learned I prepared both the company and my own personal income tax returns, Peggy started making not-so-subtle remarks questioning my sanity. One year I made a bet with her: "You do the taxes and I'll do the taxes. If you can save me more than the cost of your fee, I'll buy you the best dinner in town. If, on the other hand, the savings are less than the fee, I won't have to pay you." Peggy sure enjoyed her dinner, while I ate humble pie. Now she is a partner at another firm and only deals with the "big guys," but I still use her new firm for my taxes.

I would *strongly* suggest that you take at least one basic course in accounting, even if it's just a correspondence course, before you open the doors of your new business.

If this is your first exposure to bookkeeping, you'd be better off taking a generic course, rather than one devoted to a particular computer-based bookkeeping system. It is far better to understand the principles rather than to just learn how to push the buttons.

A basic introduction to accounting

Guess what? As if you weren't already getting enough value for your money, I'm including a general introduction to bookkeeping. What follows is not meant to take the place of a formal lesson, but at least it will start you on the path.

In your first bookkeeping lesson, you'll be introduced to a concept called "T accounts." T accounts look like this:

Cash Accounts Payable

There are five classes of accounts: **Assets, Liabilities, Equity, Income, and Expenses.** These terms mean pretty much what they say. Assets and Expenses are called "Debit Accounts"; Liabilities, Equity, and Income are "Credit Accounts." Why? They just are.

Many folks who are new to accounting are confused by the terms "debit" and "credit." These terms have a unique meaning in this context. If you remember nothing else at this point, try to recall that "**debits are on the left and credits are on the right.**" The next thing to remember is "**debits always equal credits.**" This is why it's called "**double entry bookkeeping.**" An entry on the debit side *must* have a corresponding entry on the credit side.

Additions to Debit Accounts go on the left; subtractions go on the right. Credit Accounts are treated just the opposite, with additions going on the right and subtractions going on the left. Have I lost you? Now you know why I told you to take a course. One more thing I'd like to note. The company, for purposes of accounting, is treated as a being separate from its owner(s). The company's assets are the company's, not the owner's. The owners' equity is treated sort of like a liability, payable back to the owner(s), in the event that the company is dissolved.

And so continues the lesson

In case you're stubborn and want to go further at this point, let's provide a couple of illustrations. First, say you invest $100 in your company and just let it stay there. We would debit an Asset account called Cash and credit an Equity account called, perhaps, Owner's (or Shareholder's) Equity. Our T accounts for the transaction would look something like this:

Cash		**Owner's Equity**	
100.00			100.00

Now, say you buy $50 worth of inventory for cash. We credit Cash and debit Inventory. The T accounts would look like:

Inventory		**Cash**	
50.00			50.00

Next, let's say you sell half the inventory for $100 (because you're a smart business person). This entry gets a little more complicated since it involves two Asset accounts: Cash and Inventory. It also involves an Equity account called Net Income:

Cash		**Inventory**		**Net Income**	
100.00			50.00		50.00

See, debits *always* equal credits. Once you're doing actual bookkeeping, you'll seldom use T accounts. They're a handy way to clear up momentary confusion, especially when you're new to this. Another phrase you'll hear your teacher use is, "Always balance to Cash." **Cash**, in accounting language, includes bank accounts. You do this for the same reason you reconcile your checking account promptly each month. Start from there and make sure all of your other accounts balance to your Cash account.

Asset, Liability, and Equity accounts appear on the **Balance Sheet**. These accounts indicate, respectively, what we have, what we owe, and the difference between the two. This difference represents the owner(s)' equity in the business, which, as we said, can be positive or (darn it) negative. A negative Equity condition occurs when the business owes more than it has. This is not a good situation. Income and Expense accounts appear on the **Profit & Loss** (also called **Income and Expense**), report, duh! This report indicates what we've taken in, what we've spent, and the difference between the two (hopefully, a profit.) A **Cash-flow** report is sort of a combination of the two.

Other terms you will be introduced to in your accounting course are **journal** and **ledger**, which bring to mind an image of Bob Cratchett hunched over Scrooge's records. A journal is a record of transactions; the most frequently used one being the **cash journal**, which is another name for the check register. A ledger is really a compilation of T accounts, showing the debits and credits of each transaction. You'll also hear the terms **general** and **subsidiary**, referring to both journals and ledgers. They mean pretty much what they say, general referring to the company as a whole and subsidiary dealing with particular accounts or groups of accounts. One big advantage of the computerized systems is that much of this is taken care of for you, eliminating many repetitive entries.

Since the days I was doing Bancard's books on green-ruled paper (the origin of the term, "spreadsheet"), the cost of accounting software has gone down considerably and the quality has improved substantially. Doing the books still requires a basic understanding of accounting, but the new programs can make the job much more efficient and produce a pretty good result. There are a number of products on the market. I am most familiar with Quick Books, from Intuit. I currently use it to keep track of several small companies and non-profit organizations I'm involved with. The program is easy to learn and is pretty flexible. Regardless of what it says on the side of the box, you need to know the basics of accounting before you plunge ahead.

A brief word about income and other taxes: I certainly don't intentionally pay any more in taxes than I have to. The IRS doesn't expect me to. I approach tax reporting aggressively. If there's a question, I'm going to do what's best for me. *But,* and this is important, I am going to make sure I have supporting documentation available and a good argument to back up my decision.

There's always a temptation to "forget" various items of income. *Don't give in to temptation*!!! You can argue with an IRS agent about the legitimacy of an expense item. Sometimes you'll win the argument and sometimes you'll lose. However, "overlooking" income can have nasty repercussions for you. You or your attorney may be discussing this "overlooked" income in an IRS hearing or in court some day. You really don't want that.

We've covered a lot here and you're bound to have more questions. I've just scratched the surface on this topic. You will want to read some books, take some courses, and consult with a professional, as appropriate.

Sales—Look Out! He's Trying to Sell You Something

I'll probably devote more space to this than to the other leadership functions. I've been selling for most of my life. I firmly believe that "Nothing happens in business until somebody sells something." I used to irritate the "inside" folks at Bancard by insisting, "The Company is a train, and while all the cars are important, the sales force is the engine."

Most of this section will deal with "outside," off-premise sales. Much of it will be applicable to "large-ticket" sales made on-premise, and some can even apply to relatively quick retail-store-type sales. Use what you can.

No matter how good your product or service is, someone's got to peddle it to the public. Test question: Who's the top salesperson at Microsoft? If you answered "Mr. Bill," give yourself a gold star. And this is the case with every successful company. The boss must believe strongly enough in what the company offers to sell it at every possible occasion. If the boss doesn't feel this way, why should anyone else have faith in the company's product?

Before you can make the sale, however, you need to find the right person to sell to. There is no point telling your story to someone who can't make the deal.

Back when I was peddling hospital supplies at Tetra, I learned a valuable lesson. Through trial and error, I discovered that, generally speaking, the *last* person we wanted to call on was the obvious one, the one with the title of "purchasing agent." In those days, that job seemed to have just slightly more status than the janitor. Purchasing agents generally bought exactly what the doctors and nurses (especially the nursing supervisors) told them to buy. The purchasing agent was pretty much just a conduit for orders. My job, then, was to circumvent the purchasing agents and get directly to the MD and RN decision-makers. Obviously, this did not make a whole lot of friends for me with the PAs. It's not always easy to find and get to the right person, the decision-maker, but it's the only way to get the job done.

I remember one time I wended my way out of the bowels of a hospital up to the surgical suite and outside the office of the Operating Room Supervisor, I heard her secretary tell her, "Some 'salesman' wants to see you." She assumed I was in the purchasing agent's office or down in the lobby. She told the secretary, "Tell him you can't locate me."

The secretary said, "But he's right outside your door." Not having much choice at this point, the exalted personage sighed and said, "Oh, well, I guess I have to see him." I forget whether I got the order, but at least I got that far.

The best salespeople don't really "sell" in the usual sense of the word. What they do is more like consulting. The ones who take home six- and even seven-figure paychecks have spent significant time and effort discovering *why* people would want or need their product or service. They research *who and where these people are* and how to make these prospects *aware of their wants and needs*. Finally, they determine how to help their customers *satisfy these needs*, by using their product or service.

If you feel your selling skills might need a little sharpening, I'd suggest you read some books or attend some seminars on the subject. I mention a few later on in this book. Check the Internet for more. Obviously, some are better than others. You might ask some of your salesperson acquaintances for recommendations. Even if you intend to hire a sales manager, you'd better know enough about selling to keep him or her on track. Also, you'll need to have the sales skills required to participate in the really big deals.

A Word or Two on Negotiating

This, also, is the subject of books and seminars, but we'll touch on it. We could have put this just about anywhere in this or the next chapter. While negotiating is a part of selling, it is applicable almost anywhere in business. Most of us have had some experience in this art during the process of buying a car. You were trying to pay no more than you had to while the salesperson was trying to maximize the selling price and, most likely, the commission. While the term "negotiating" is seldom applied to card games, the skills are similar. You don't know what cards the car salesperson is holding (the rock-bottom price). He or she can't (hopefully) see your cards (the most you're willing to pay).

Probably the first rule in negotiating is: **Try to negotiate from strength**. If you can effectively stack the cards in your favor before you begin, you have a big head start. While bluffing can work, you've got a lot better chance of winning if you really do hold the cards. Going back to the car-buying situation, you can determine the dealer's approximate cost on various websites. This leads us to Rule 2: **Don't give away your true objective**—final price, in this example. And Rule 3: **Try, as quickly as possible, to determine the other person's true objective.** The person who can accomplish this first has a tremendous advantage. You know the point at which the other person will walk away from the deal. Attempting to negotiate beyond that point is futile. We'll mention negotiating again when we discuss business ethics.

You may or may not be aware of the fact that you can sometimes negotiate a better price on a purchase in a store, particularly a large purchase. The key here, again, is finding someone who can actually make a decision to lower the price, often the owner or a senior manager. One of my neighbors looks for slightly damaged goods, such as an open bag of fertilizer. I can't believe what he ends up paying for stuff I would have bought at full price.

And here is probably the best tool ever for negotiating: When the other guy mentions his price, you open your eyes wide and scream, "Arrgh!" or "Oh-my-god!" Then shut up and wait for him to come back with a better deal. You can laugh, but it works. Try it next time you get the chance.

We will spend more time, *a lot more time*, on the subject of selling in Chapter Three, which covers actual operation of your company.

Support—"If You Can't Be an Athlete, Then Be an Athletic Supporter"

When I use the term "support," I am referring to all functions of the business other than management, production, and sales.

"Customer support" is one important example. We have already agreed who the most important person in your business is, right? Who did you say? The customer; exactly. And what does this important person want and expect from "his" business? You've got it: satisfaction. The customer wants to be satisfied that the product or service will live up to (or, preferably, exceed) his or her expectations. And the customer wants to be satisfied that, should it not perform satisfactorily, someone will do something about it: fix it, replace it, or take it back.

It is essential that all of your people, especially your first-line customer-contact people, buy into this idea. Their jobs (and your job) depend on keeping the customer happy. Someone once said that a satisfied customer will tell two or three friends while a dissatisfied one will tell anyone who will listen. Another way of putting it is the saying attributed to Abraham Lincoln: "You can fool some of the people all of the time, and all of the people some of the time, but you cannot fool all of the people all of the time." If you're trying to make do with shoddy customer service, you're trying to fool people, and eventually this will backfire on you.

I believe both these statements, and if you expect your business to grow and prosper, you'd better believe them, too. This is especially true if your business, as most do, depends on repeat customers.

At Bancard, our customer service folks were authorized, on their own, *without asking anyone*, to do anything the customer wanted up to a cost limit of $100. Our first-level supervisors had a higher limit, and so on.

This doesn't mean you have to give away the store. Also at Bancard, we had a mythical graph we called the PITA graph, which had nothing to do with Greek bread. Those initials stood for "Pain In The A—." We semi-jokingly graphed each customer with two lines: one labeled "Revenue" and the other labeled "Aggravation." When the "A" line rose above the "R" line, the customer was to receive a polite hint to take his business somewhere else. Understand, the PITA Graph existed only in our imaginations. What did exist was a customer-grading system based primarily on how much revenue each customer brought in. All of our customers were treated with courtesy, but the "A's" got first priority, followed by the "B's" and then the "C's." We had some pretty difficult "A's," but we took really good care of them.

Many companies boast about "excellent customer service" but few, especially the larger ones, really provide it. Think about it; when was the last time you were left with a warm feeling after a contact with a company? This is especially true when you have a complaint. As I mentioned previously, one of my pet gripes is the increasingly pervasive automated phone-answering system. When you finally guess at the selection you want, you get the message, "We're sorry, but all our representatives are busy helping [really important] customers" (so you, you poor sucker, can just sit and wait for your neck to cramp up).

How did that make you feel, the last time you heard this type of message? Were you eager to keep doing business with this company? This is not my idea of "excellent customer service." In a *Wall Street Journal* article of May 22, 2002, Mark Reidel, the vice president of operations for Frederick's of Hollywood, is quoted as saying, "Customer service to me is the worst job in the world. I couldn't do it." Personally, I think this is a lousy attitude. Unfortunately for us as customers, this attitude appears to be standard operating procedure at many businesses.

Had I ever thought of patronizing Frederick's (for my wife, of course), Mr. Reidel's comment would go a long way toward changing my mind. How do you think his attitude affects the people who handle customer service at his company? He's playing right into the hands of Victoria's Secret.

So how can we, as entrepreneurs, differentiate ourselves from the herd? We can imbue our people with the Milking Stool philosophy and the Circular Organization Chart concept. As a result, we'll have a big leg up on competition.

Okay, how are you going to encourage *your* people to truly give "excellent customer service"?

First, set an example. If your people see you being rude to or ignoring a troublesome customer, what message will they get from that?

Second, provide them with the incentive to do it right. If they have control over all or part of their compensation and they understand how the level of service they provide affects their pay, they'll figure it out.

How do you accomplish this? Let's go back and look at the job description. Does it contain individual and team goals and standards? What happens if they meet these goals? What happens if they exceed them? If the company benefits from their hard work, shouldn't they share in the rewards on a monthly or paycheck-by-paycheck basis? What do they have to do to get promoted? Do they *know* what they have to do?

One thing to consider—how is their bonus or other incentive affected if they or their department do well and the company still does poorly? You will want to structure the incentive so that they have some control over it but so that it also reflects the results of the company as a whole.

If you get nothing else from this chapter, paste this on your computer monitor:

"It costs a whole lot less to keep a customer than it does to get a new one."

Stare at this message as often as you can, with time out for meals, of course.

Beyond Customer Service—Additional Support Functions

Other support functions that you may need to handle include Information Technology, Purchasing, Housekeeping, and so on. You may be able to outsource some of these. Except in a fairly large company, IT is a good candidate for outsourcing. Computers work very well—when they work. When they don't, you'd best have someone on tap who knows what he or she is doing. We were very fortunate in having two IT people who not only knew what they were doing but also were able to relate to the rest of us dummies. You may be able to contract with your computer vendor for ongoing service, or you might find a knowledgeable service firm.

Housekeeping and Maintenance are other possible candidates for outsourcing. I don't know about you, but I'd just as soon outsource the mopping and the dusting. What's more, if water starts shooting out of the bathroom sink, I don't want to interrupt a call with a customer to deal with the problem.

Purchasing may or may not be assigned to your accounting department. Sloppy purchasing practices can punch a big hole in your bottom line. It is best to limit purchasing authority to one or two people who can review requests and requisitions, determine their validity, and determine where and how to fulfill them. These people should be charged with pre-approval of all vendors' invoices, prior to payment. Here, again, the Internet is a great source of information to help with purchasing. There's a site called bizrate.com, among others, that lists prices and vendors for various products. It also gives them ratings, reflecting the quality of service.

We've already covered some of the other support functions—Human Resources and Accounting—in their own sections. Just remember, no team survives without the proper support. It's part of your job to make certain that each of these vital services is properly covered at your business.

Nuts and Bolts—The Little Things That Hold Your Business Together

If you've not already done so, I strongly suggest you take a moment to visit the web site of the Small Business Administration (www.sba.gov.).

This site touches on many of the subjects we cover in this book, sometimes from a different viewpoint. Check out the various services offered by the SBA, almost all without charge to you (other than the taxes you've paid to support it.) One possibly valuable resource is their Service Core of Retired Executives (SCORE). These are people experienced in business who volunteer their time and expertise solely to help people like you and me start and manage our businesses. Be aware, however, that they *are* volunteers and it is up to you to evaluate the advice you are given and your relationship with a particular SCORE counselor.

Another source of help you might pursue is the business department of a nearby college or university. Faculty members sometimes make themselves available for consulting, usually for a fee. Also, some schools have an intern program, offering undergraduate or graduate students to perform various tasks as part of their curriculum.

In this section, we'll cover briefly some of the "things" you may need in your operation. We'll go over just the basics, as many of these things will vary from business to business. Just as with your particular product or service, we'll assume you know more about the details than I do.

The first thing that comes to mind is a computer. Despite your grandma's disdain for new-fangled things, trying to do business without an adequate computer system is futile. If you already own a computer and you're happy with it, fine. It can do double duty. Two things to consider: If the computer is at home and the business isn't, you may want to spring for another one. Second, in order to deduct or depreciate a computer, the IRS wants it used *solely* for business. If you should happen to get audited and the examiner finds personal correspondence or games on the hard drive, he or she might disallow the deduction. I expect, though, that they might be a little more lenient nowadays, since many people use their computers both at work and at home. Having jpegs of your cat on your computer might not, of itself, disqualify the deduction. It's your choice. Another thought: If your home computer utilizes an operating system other than Microsoft's Windows, you might consider switching. Apple and LINUX have their fans, but for the time being, there are far more business applications written for Windows. People tend to have strong feelings, pro and con, about Microsoft. However, their lead here is so great that you're really swimming against the tide if you don't use a Windows-based machine. If you are getting a new machine, get the fastest and best one you can afford. Be sure the machine has enough memory, both RAM and hard drive. This will provide some "upgrade insurance" to support your growing business.

To make the computer useful, you'll need software. For your business, consider buying an office suite, such as Microsoft Office or Corel WordPerfect. Office suites typically combine a number of useful programs, including word-processing, presentations software, spreadsheet, and database. As I mentioned earlier, you will probably also want to purchase one of the basic accounting programs. Give some thought, if you need a cash register, to one that is PC-based and can be networked into your office machine. If you have limited computer knowledge, get expert help. This can save a lot of time and grief.

Your computer may come packaged with a printer. If not, you will need one. Depending on their features, inkjet printers often cost less and are fine for most work. Laser printers deliver a little more quality and speed. Laser printer toner should cost less than ink-jet cartridges, especially if you will be printing many pages.

You will need the ability to send and receive faxes. E-mails presently cannot handle signatures. You can do this with software and a scanner, a dedicated fax machine, or a "combo" or multi-function machine. Be wary of machines that come too cheap. Many companies are "giving away razors so they can sell the blades." I would suggest that you stick with one of the major brands. Try to make sure the maintenance costs of the unit you buy won't be a burden. With some of the lower-priced machines, it no longer pays to perform much service. The cost of fixing them often equals or exceeds the cost of replacing them.

There are several excellent multi-function units available. These devices combine several of the following functions: black and white printer, color printer, fax, copier, and scanner. One problem: If the multi-function unit goes down, you lose all your capabilities, not just one. Also, while it's performing one job, it may not be available for others. If you're anticipating a lot of copying, for instance, a separate copier might be a better choice.

I would suggest you specify universal service bus (USB 2.0) connection for all of your computer accessories or peripherals. These fast, easy, and flexible connections have become the standard for device connection.

Okay, now I know what to buy. How do I pay for all this great stuff?

For much of your business equipment, you will have the choice of leasing or buying. Consider the advantages and disadvantages of each. Leasing may seem like the way to go, especially when your budget is limited. Leasing generally involves low up-front costs, and the lease payments may not have to be carried on your books as a liability. If the lease agreement is properly worded, the entire payment should be deductible on your tax return. On the other hand, leasing companies are not charitable organizations. They, like you, are in business to make money. You will generally pay much more over the life of the lease than you would if you bought the equipment outright. I once calculated the lease payments as providing the leasing company a *33 percent annual return* on the price of the equipment! Consider budgeting the cash cost of the equipment and adding it to your start-up capital. Or, if the purchase can be put off for a while, "save" for it out of profits. Even if you have to borrow the money to buy something, you'll probably pay far less interest to the bank than you would to a leasing company. One woman told me that, at the end of the lease term, during which she had already paid several times the cash purchase cost, she had to return the equipment or pay an exorbitant "buy-out" fee.

One exception to the above advice might be a large copier or other complex piece of equipment. On these, service contracts are often bundled in with a lease, and you *will* need service on these on a regular basis. In any case, read before you sign.

I strongly suggest, even if you're running a home business, that you set up at least one separate phone line. This should never be answered by family members, with "Hello." It's a business phone and a lifeline to your customers. If you cannot be available at all times, consider an answering machine, an answering service or forwarding your calls to a cell phone. With the decreasing cost of cell-phone service, you might want to use your cell as your primary business phone. That's what I am doing presently. Another option is a "virtual office." We'll have more to say on this later. If you're going to be online a lot of the time, or if more than one person will need to use the phone simultaneously, you should consider additional lines. Now that Ma Bell no longer controls things, you can shop around for both local and long distance service. You might, at first, "forget" to tell your carrier that it will be a business line, unless you need Yellow Pages advertising.

How do I get paid?

Avoid selling on credit if you can. Doctors, for instance, used to bill for services once a month. I guess some still do.

Most medical offices nowadays display a sign to the effect of "Payment Is Expected at Time of Service."

You might want to consider accepting credit card payments for your goods or services. More and more businesses, not just retailers, are accepting "plastic" nowadays. People have grown used to the convenience and extras (airline miles, rebates, discounts on car purchases) associated with the cards. Large companies and federal, state, and local governments have found that using credit cards for purchases, especially smaller ones, allows them to avoid the purchase order process and save time and money.

Many companies provide their employees with credit cards, rather than expense accounts. You'll probably want to cash in on this trend and provide your customers with payment options.

No matter what your business—whether it's retail, food service, wholesale, manufacturing, or service—you need to consider whether accepting this type of payment might bring you more business.

When I started in the credit card business in 1980, card receipts comprised a small portion of payments for many businesses. These days, it is not uncommon for plastic to constitute the bulk of their receipts.

If you do decide to take credit cards, find a processor or bank and complete your application well before your start date. Approval can take anywhere from several days to several weeks. Be aware that both the type and cost of credit card equipment and the "discount" or rate you pay are negotiable. Don't, however, be lured by apparent low price alone. Sometimes you get what you pay for. This will be an ongoing service. It will depend on a number of things working right: your equipment, your phone connection to your processor, and the processor's computer system. Most of the time, the system will work fine, if it is properly set up in the first place. When something goes wrong, you'll want to have confidence in your provider that they will get you back up and running quickly so that your business isn't impacted.

As with any other outside service you'll be considering, check around. Get references and call them. A good credit card relationship can be a godsend; a bad one can be a nightmare. Go back to Chapter One and read the part about the scum that has been attracted to this industry. Read the fine print in the contract and **delete any reference to a termination penalty**. If your processor doesn't perform satisfactorily, then you should be free to change without a penalty. You will want to accept MasterCard and Visa, at a minimum. American Express, Diners Club, and Discover generally charge more. Most people who have one of these last cards also have a Visa or a MasterCard. A competent credit card sales and service organization should be able to set you up to accept any of the cards you want to accept.

Watch out for a quoted unrealistic low rate tied in with an exorbitant equipment cost. This is often tied in with a lease. I have seen lease payments of more than $50 a month for up to five years. This comes to $3000 on a piece of equipment that might cost $800 or so if purchased for cash from a more reputable company. And they still didn't own it at the end of the lease term. The salesperson and the selling company couldn't care less if you stay with them after they raised your rate; you're still stuck with the lease payments and they've pocketed the profit.

If you will be utilizing the Internet as a sales and marketing tool, you'll need to set up and maintain a website. It's not rocket science, but you may need qualified assistance, especially at first. Consider this as carefully as you do your location, signage, and other advertising. If your site will be a principal method of contact between you and your customers, you will want it to be as inviting and customer-friendly as your physical location, if you have one. The first issue to consider: How will your customers locate your site? Will you advertise with banner ads? Will you list yourself with various search engines? Bear in mind that it doesn't matter how great your site is if people don't know about it. Getting placement on the various search engines is a subject unto itself. The larger ones charge both for listing and positioning.

Where's everyone going to sit?

The type and quality of furniture and fixtures you need will depend on the nature and location of your business and the amount of on-site client contact you expect. If appearance is critical, you may want to engage the services of an interior designer. If, on the other hand, saving a buck is your first priority, consider alternate sources. Used furniture stores often have attractive pieces at prices considerably lower than new furniture. If you like auctions, and have a pretty good idea of what you want and what you should pay for it, you might consider this route. Watch the want ads in your local papers for companies going out of business, remodeling, or contracting out their operations.

Shopping the Internet, of course, is another option for either auctions or direct sales. I recently needed an under-desk tray for a laptop. When I tried to buy one at Comp USA and Office Max, the salespeople looked at me as if I were crazy. A quick search of the Net turned up a vendor that had exactly what I was looking for.

Depending on your anticipated mail volume, you may want to invest in a postage meter. Be aware that several companies make these. You can compare the features and prices of the various models. You also can subscribe to services that allow you to print postage on your own computer. These services have limitations and special requirements, however, and may not be suitable for everyone.

Cubicles with movable walls are the hot things at the moment, and workers seem to have accommodated themselves pretty well to working in them. These offer the advantage of flexibility and permit efficient use of space. People have begun to think of their cubicle as their office. This has its advantages and disadvantages. Without a door to close, everyone is sharing the same airspace. My son works at a company full of computer programmers. He's mentioned to me that a few of these folks talk both loudly and often, both on the phone and to one another. Should you consider this layout, keep in mind the potential effect on employee morale and the quality of work.

Alternatives are open offices and traditional offices with walls. Spend some time considering what will work for you. Take into account anticipated growth and changes in operations.

If you've followed the suggestions and consulted the recommended sources in this chapter, you should be about ready to get your new enterprise underway. The next section of the book should help you get it up to speed and keep it on course.

When *Should* You Quit Your Day Job?

In a May 7, 2002, article, *The Wall Street Journal* provides this checklist for when to cut the cord. It makes sense to me, so I've included it. The author is Tom Kinnear, a professor at the University of Michigan's business school. He lists the following:

1. The co-founders have invested money.
2. Angels or other investors are ready to invest
3. Potential customers are ready to buy the product.
4. Potential employees are ready to sign on.
5. The product is based on serious intellectual property—and it actually works.

All the above are important, but I think the most important thing is to have customers who are **ready to buy**. The fact that they like it will not guarantee widespread demand for it.

CHAPTER THREE

Tending Your Garden—Starting and Making It Grow

Leadership—Some Writers Still Call It Management

In this chapter we're going to cover much of the same ground we've already explored, but we'll go into greater detail and examine things from a different perspective. The emphasis will shift from planning to doing. In the formative stage of the company you (and your partners, if any) will probably be what my dad used to call "chief cook and bottle washers." In other words, you will need to be able to perform, or closely supervise, every aspect of the company.

We've alluded to leadership several times, but it's so important to a company's success that I want to begin this chapter of the book with an in-depth discussion of it. Volumes have been written on this subject. They've described leaders in all types of enterprises, from Biblical times to today: statesmen, religious leaders, coaches, generals, and captains of industry. A chapter, even a long one, can be only the beginning.

You'll want to have a well-handled *anonymous* suggestion box at your company. Suggestions from your staff can elicit valuable insight into your performance as a leader, as well as many other things. While an open-door policy is a good thing, many people don't have the confidence to express really sensitive topics in front of the boss. They tend to assume that "anything you say, can and will be used against you." An anonymous suggestion box provides a means for employees to express themselves without having to edit their thoughts.

It is important, though, to provide feedback for the suggestions, even the anonymous ones. One method for accomplishing this would be to post a periodic list of the suggestions on the company bulletin board, along with the reasons why they are or are not being instituted.

I've mentioned that the key to a good company is good people. The key to having motivated, productive people is a good leader. I make no claim to special expertise on this subject, but I'll share with you what I've read, what I've observed, and what has worked for me.

Above all, a good leader has to inspire people. By this, I don't mean wearing a white robe, sporting a halo, and standing on a pedestal. We are all human; we all make mistakes. Your people will forgive most of these mistakes, as you will forgive theirs. I think it was Harry Truman, again, who had a sign reading, "A turtle never makes progress unless its neck is out." If fear of failure keeps you from trying, your accomplishments will be limited. When you make a mistake, the thing to do is admit it, apologize, if appropriate, and make it right.

You have two basic choices in running the company. You can stand behind your folks with a whip and scream at them, "Faster, faster!" Or, you get out in front, wave your sword, and cry "Charge!" Which of these sounds like a better approach to you?

First and foremost, you must have a vision for the company and you must make certain that each and every employee knows and understands that vision. What is it you're trying to accomplish? How do you plan on reaching your goal? Although a business needs to make a profit to stay in business, making a lot of money for yourself is just not an appropriate vision. It's got to be bigger than that. How are you going to change the world or, at least, your little part of it? Where does each employee fit into the vision? How can he/she help (or hurt) the plan?

Second, you need to set an example. If you cut corners and treat other people like dirt, what does that tell your associates? My grandfather used to say (in jest, I hope), "Do as I say, not as I do." That won't work today, if it ever did. Far be it from me to try to improve on a good thing, but I tend to use as a guide what I call the Golden Rule version 2.0.This states: "**Do unto others as *they* would be done to.**" Get to know your people and find out what's important to them. Show them that you know and care about what's important to them and act accordingly.

Although I have served on a number of boards and committees, I have typically not shone in this setting. I function best in a linear situation where I have a boss (the ultimate bosses are the customers) and others report to me. This does not mean I get to say, "Do it because I tell you to." People who do things because they have to just don't perform as well as folks who do things because they want to and believe they're doing the right thing. You will need to keep building consensus and keep everyone on the same page. If you've hired and kept the best people, each will have something to contribute. A wise leader takes full advantage of these contributions.

One technique that's worked for me is to ask each person who comes to me with a problem to have, in advance, one or two solutions. I would answer the question "What should we do?" with my own question: "What do you think might work?" After a while, folks got the idea and would come prepared. Often, they weren't looking for my brilliant ideas on something they knew a whole lot better than I did. Instead, they wanted confirmation of their instincts and support of their ideas.

What I said earlier about taking responsibility for your actions applies to their actions as well. You'll want to encourage each of them to become mini-entrepreneurs, not just robots. If they come up with a better way to do their job, who wins? You do. "Better," of course, like beauty, is in the eye of the beholder. You'll need to be able to distinguish between the useful and the impracticable. Praise, accept and utilize the useful ideas. Thank the person who submitted the unusable suggestion, explain why it won't work, and encourage him or her to try again. Avoid, at all costs, the NIH (Not Invented Here) syndrome. Good ideas can come from anyone; just because an idea wasn't yours doesn't mean you should treat it lightly.

The good, the not so good, and the in-between

It is a given fact that any group of people (your employees, your customers, or your friends, for example) can be divided into three sub-groups, the super, the good, and the rest. We mentioned the P.I.T.A. graph we had in our minds for rating the customers. You remember what P.I.T.A. stood for? For the employees, let's consider the Bell Curve, a concept that can be useful in many situations. With a little effort, you will be able to place your people somewhere along the curve. Jack Welch, in his book "*Jack, From the Gut*," tells us that General Electric calls it the Vitality Curve, and places 20 percent of the people at the top, 10 percent at the bottom, and the remaining 70 percent in between. You can come up with your own percentage formula, but the concept still applies.

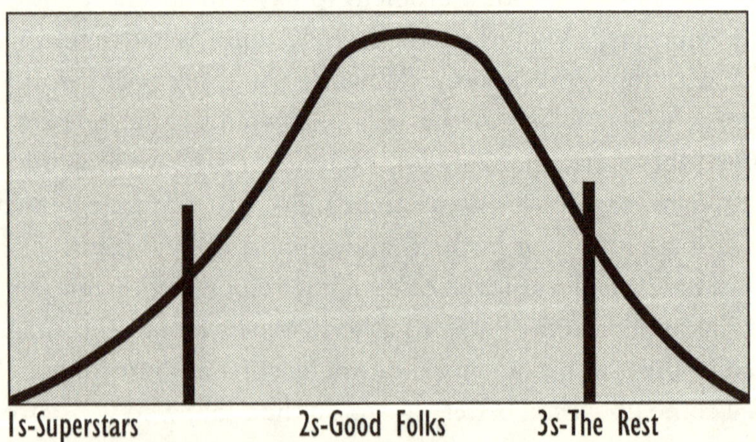

Of these three, which will you want to give the most attention to? 1s? Wrong. 3s? Sorry. And that leaves the 2s. Why? Let's see.

Your superstars will pretty much take care of themselves. They're motivated, dedicated, self-starters. You'll want to love 'em, bonus 'em, promote 'em, and hang on to them. These are the ones the headhunters will be after. You need to head off the hunters by making your shop the best possible place to work. What to do with the 3s? Get rid of them as fast and as humanely as you can. You aren't doing them or your company or the employees any favor by hanging on to them. You know what they say about bad apples. And, in fact, they may be more suited for another job at another company. As always, you need to be on firm ground, morally and legally, when you terminate someone. We will be discussing this in greater detail in the H.R. and Legal sections of the book.

Okay, now about the 2s. These people make up the bulk of your force. They are the ones who will make or break you. They're conscientious and good at their jobs. Your task, should you care to accept it (and you'd better), is to bring them along to become as close to the 1s as possible. How? Let's go back to the job description and mission statement. Are you sure they understand them? Have they bought-in? Do they know what their goals are? Do they know how to reach them?

In addition to his or her immediate supervisor, each employee should have a mentor. The mentor's goal is to get that person from a 2 to a 1. Except in rare cases, the employee should be assured that anything said to the mentor will go no further. Sort of like a doctor/patient relationship. Each employee should have a scheduled review at no more than six-month and preferably three-month intervals. Part of a supervisor's performance review should address the mentor role. How is he or she doing? What is he or she doing right? What is he or she doing wrong? How has the supervisor helped the individual during this period? What is the supervisor or mentor going to do to help him or her next period?

At General Electric, according to Jack Welch, reviews were conducted not only on a top-down basis but each manager also received reviews from his/her peers and *subordinates.* As Robert Burns wrote:

Oh, would some power the giftee give us/To see ourselves as others see us.

Carrying this one step further, you will also want to conduct a periodic review of one other person—yourself. The suggestion box can help. Another technique is to make reviewing *you* part of each of your senior people's review. Watch out for sucking up, though. Make it clear that you want to hear the whole story, the good and the bad, and there had better be some bad.

A piece of advice about giving advice

Will you want to get involved with your people's personal lives? You won't want to, but it will be inevitable. This is especially true with those with whom you work closely and with other long-term employees. In an ideal work world, folks would leave their family and personal problems outside the plant door, but I've never seen the ideal. Problems at home inevitably affect the way people do their jobs. One of the skills you'll develop is knowing what you can help with, when to bring in outside help, and when to butt out.

Unless you've been trained as a social worker or counselor of some sort, getting too involved in these types of problems can be like stepping on a landmine. Listen, by all means, but be wary of giving gratuitous advice. Know when to suggest a trained outsider—a clergyman, a doctor, or a counselor of some sort. You might check around your community to see just what sort of help is available so that you'll be prepared.

Another path to tread lightly with your folks is the financial one. Even if they are paid a fair wage, some will inevitably encounter money problems from time to time. Where will they turn for help? To the boss, of course. My suggestion here is to resist the temptation to loan or advance funds in most cases. From *Macbeth*, my dad used to echo Polonius's advice to Laertes, his son:

"Neither a borrower nor a lender be, for a loan oft loses both itself and friend."

Take a moment to read the text under EMPLOYEE ADVANCES in the sample Employee Manual I've included in the Appendix. Does this policy sound heartless to you? Perhaps it is. Some people, unfortunately, will not be grateful that you or the company got them out of a hole. They will resent that they had to humble themselves and ask. They may even resent you for being in a position to make the loan.

This lesson was brought home to me in the case of my last administrative assistant. Among other things, I made her a substantial no-interest loan to bail her parents out of a tough spot. A fire had destroyed their store and they were having trouble collecting the insurance. She did pay back the loan but later went out of her way to aggravate an already difficult situation. After we had merged the company, my new bosses and I began having differences. In her perception of the way the wind was then blowing, my "assistant" abandoned all pretense of loyalty. She chose to forget whom she was supposed to be assisting.

On the other hand, if a key employee is facing a real crisis, you might want to help. You also might consider making the donation anonymously. We did this when the son of one of our top salespeople was diagnosed with leukemia. We made a substantial contribution through his church. To this day, he is probably unaware of our help. And that's fine.

Substance abuse, alcohol or drugs of any kind, can wreak havoc with your business. Believe me; in this case, both the victim and you need professional help. Don't try to manage a drunk or a drug addict by yourself. Too often, the only remedy, for the company, is to terminate the individual before the problem affects too many other people. You did include in your personnel manual a provision against the use of drugs and alcohol on company premises and when on company business, didn't you?

In all my supervisory positions, when I had an office door, it was always open, except when privacy was critical. Unlike a person whom my son, Steve, once worked for, when I said the door was open, I meant it. And everyone in the company knew it. When I was introduced to a new employee, my standard speech went something like this: "If you have a problem or want to discuss something, please take it up with your supervisor. If you and your supervisor can't work it out, take it to your boss's boss, and up the line, if necessary. Finally, as you can see, this door is open, but the first question I'm going to ask is, 'Did you discuss this with your boss? What did he or she say?'" If necessary, we would bring the boss in to join our discussion.

A few more thoughts on LEADING your business

It is tempting and, perhaps, only natural to think of you and the company as one and the same. Resist this temptation, as best you can. There will be times when you need to choose. What is best for the company may not be the ideal thing for you, at least in the short term. Here are two instances:

You are short a few bucks for that new car you want, so you might want to take an unscheduled distribution. On the other hand, that money would pay for a new hire or piece of equipment that would make the business run better for some time to come. Even more critical, it would help to pay a large bill to a supplier within terms. Ignore that little horned guy on your shoulder and do the right thing. I can't count the number of times Judy asked for the household money, only to be told, "Sorry, babe, it'll be a little late this month. We had to meet payroll." She heard this less and less, of course, as the companies got larger and more profitable.

Here's the other one: You really don't like Harry very much, but he's one of your key employees. This is a good time to remember the Serenity Prayer:

"Lord, give me the courage to change what I can,
The patience to accept what I cannot change,
And the wisdom to know the difference."

Until I memorized this, it was taped to my computer monitor.

Do what you can for Harry, but treat him fairly and recognize his importance to the company. Applaud his good points and help him, as best you can, to overcome the rest.

Another temptation to resist is acting like a parent to employees. The average age of the people working at Bancard was somewhere in the mid-twenties, while I had advanced into my sixties. Most of them were the contemporaries of my children and it was really hard, sometimes, not to treat them accordingly. Again, this is a bad idea. They were *not* children; they were adults and deserved to be treated like adults. They had families and mortgages, and I needed to keep in mind that I was their employer, not their father.

If I seem to give the impression that the most important job of a leader is to LEAD, guess what? It's intentional. Your people *are* your business. They are you, to the outside world.

Nowhere have I implied that leadership is easy. Oftentimes, you'll need to choose between the right way and the easy way. Your people are looking to you to wave that sword and march ahead. If they sense insecurity in you, they'll quickly falter. If, on the other hand, you lead bravely, head held high, they're more likely to follow your example.

Staffing

Let's assume that you've identified your market, specified your product or service, found a location, and secured the necessary furniture and equipment for the start-up phase. What do you do next?

Probably you'll start looking for people to help you, unless you can initially handle all aspects of the operation by yourself. By the way, starting off solo, or with a very small group, may not be a bad idea. If you get hands-on experience with all of the various tasks involved in your business, you'll be better able to train and supervise others to perform them when the time comes. The view from the top is nice, but it's important to be able to see things through your people's eyes. If you've "been there, done that," your credibility will be increased.

During the first months of Bancard, I was the negotiator, salesperson, mechanic, serviceman, bookkeeper, and whatever else was required. Several months later, I hired as "secretary" a neighbor. Her main qualification was that she lived down the street and could work as few hours as I needed. She probably typed faster than I did, but she made just as many mistakes. While she was better than nothing during the early months of the company, her skills just weren't up to the job once we got rolling. Our next part-time employee was a bookkeeper, for when I got frustrated wrestling with the spreadsheets. (In those days they were sheets of green paper, ruled off in columns and rows.)

Anyway, let's assume you're ready to hire one or more people right off. You've decided that your time would be better spent doing something other than cooking and washing bottles. How should you go about getting your new employees ramped-up quickly? How can you train them in such a way as to avoid problems later? First, as I've suggested, you'd better have a working knowledge of the jobs they're supposed to do. Next, you need to have a detailed written job description available during the first interview. As with any company document, this will not be inscribed in stone. They say, "The only constant is change." This applies here as it does with every other aspect of business. Outline the job as best you can now and be prepared to make changes as you go along. Many of the changes will reflect the input from the people who know the job best, the people doing the work.

There are many ways to attract potential employees. Word of mouth is certainly the least expensive and, in some ways, the best. If a person comes recommended by someone you know and trust, you should be ahead of the game. Who do you know that might be able to suggest someone to fill the spot? Should you offer them a reward if they do suggest a suitable candidate? Can you hire some of your ex-coworkers from your last place of employment? Naturally, you can't do this if you've signed a written agreement not to. You might place want ads in the local paper, trade publications, or on job boards on the Internet. Consider whether you are prepared to pay interview and relocation expenses. Include that in any national ad you place.

You need to avoid legal pitfalls in the hiring process. This begins with the ad you place. Federal and state laws prohibit you from even the appearance of discrimination against certain classes of people. Avoid any semblance of prejudice against "protected classes." These include but are not limited to: nationality, race, religion, gender, age, and disability. Hiring the best person for the job, as I mentioned before, should help keep you out of this kind of trouble.

Be careful what you include in your ad. Don't specify more education than you really need for the job (graduate degree, MBA, etc.) If you do this, you might preclude otherwise-qualified candidates from applying. You might also wind up paying more than necessary to fill the job. "Young, energetic" might tend to exclude older workers. I can think of no reason to specify gender. Even with regard to heavy lifting, some women can outperform many men. Try to keep the wording of the ad focused on the job itself.

Okay, you've gotten the word out and the resumes are coming in. How do you narrow the responses to a manageable group of interviews? Speed-reading is helpful but, with a little practice, you will learn to skim the resumes, eliminate the BS, and focus on the important parts: What do the candidates say they can offer you in terms of job performance? Are they focused on what they want in a job or, more importantly, on how they can help your growing company? I am leery of resumes that reflect job-hopping. Someone who has moved every few months is probably not inclined to stay with you, either, for any period of time. Hiring and training, as you are about to find out, consumes time and money. I would probably circular-file any resume with job-change periods averaging less than two years, unless they have exceptional qualifications or darned good reasons for changing jobs.

Depending on the complexity of the position and on what else you have to do, you might schedule interviews at one- or two-hour intervals, or you might want to do no more than one or two a day. A friend once interviewed for a company where they booked him with back-to-back interviews every half hour for a full day. What you'd end up with, with that kind of performance, would be a bunch of bits and pieces from each interviewer, probably all different.

I often found myself tempted, in an interview, to spend too much time talking and not enough time listening and observing the candidate. Sure, you want to sell the company and the position, but your main task here is to discover, as early in the process as possible, whether or not this person is the right fit for the job and for the company, both now and in the future.

Think back on the times when you were the candidate. What were you doing? You were selling yourself. Assuming you wanted or needed the job, you put on your best face. Didn't you succumb to the temptation to puff yourself a little? Did you, perhaps, leave out a few negatives?

The person across the table from you now is probably no different than you were then. Your job is to try to see through the veneer and discover the real positives and negatives. This is not easy, but you get better at it with practice.

Assuming the person has had an opportunity to read the job description, your first task will be to put him or her at ease. Smile, make a few general comments and ask a few general questions. "Did you have any trouble finding us?" "Do you think it's too warm in here?" Offering a soft drink or water can both help to put the person at ease and give you a chance to observe multi-taking skills. While you're doing this, take a few moments to refresh yourself on the applicant's resume, which you have read previously. Next, pick out a few significant points in the resume and ask for further clarification. Listen carefully to the answers and *observe the body language.* Often that will tell you more than the words being said.

Perhaps the next step would be to ask, "Why would you like to work for this particular company? And "Why do you think you are suitable for this position?" Again, listen and watch carefully, and make notes of significant points. Avoid getting adversarial. I worked with a board member of a non-profit organization who quickly put the interviewee on the defensive. I think this caused us to miss out on some likely candidates. Also, try to avoid asking too many "standard interview questions." People tend to rehearse their answers to these.

If you are interviewing candidates for a sales position, you might set up a hypothetical sales situation and ask the person to try to sell you something. Interviewing for other positions might involve a brief test of skills, such as typing or computer knowledge. Once, when I was trying to fill a C.F.O. slot, I asked each candidate who survived the first interview to come back with a brief business plan for a situation closely paralleling ours. The candidates brought in a wide range of plans. This helped quite a bit with the final hiring decision.

You can stop the hiring process at any time, but be very careful to treat each candidate equally. Do not do anything or say anything that might be considered prejudicial. Questions you *cannot* ask include such seemingly innocent-sounding ones as, "How old are you?", "Do you have children?", "What country are you from?", "How did you become disabled?". Asking any of these could come back to bite you. A person who didn't get the job could later claim that your hiring process was prejudiced. What's worse, the government might be paying their legal bills while you'd have to pay your own. Keep the conversation as job-specific as possible.

When you have selected your final candidate, current practice is to send or give him or her a written job offer. Keep this brief, but attach the job description, state the rate and basis of pay (hourly or salary), and describe the working conditions. Unless a contract will be involved (and this is usually not advisable), include a statement that this is an "employment at will" position that may be terminated at the company's discretion. Ask the employee to sign a copy as evidence of acceptance. In the event that you do have to fire someone, make sure to document the reasons leading up to termination. If an employee can make a case that you violated his or her civil rights, then you might still be liable for an action.

Let's spend a few moments explaining the difference between an "employee" and an "independent contractor." From an accounting perspective, you need to withhold and pay taxes (including Social Security, Unemployment, and Workman's Compensation) for an employee. On the other hand, an independent contractor is responsible for his or her own taxes. The IRS, naturally, would rather collect from you and, accordingly, has set strict rules as to who qualifies as an independent contractor. Generally, an independent contractor will work out of his or her own facility, set his or her own hours, not receive specific task directions from the company, and may work for more than one employer at a time. Check the current regulations on this, but if any of these don't apply, the person must be treated as an employee.

You need to file tax form 1099-MISC for any independent contractor to whom you paid more than $600 in a calendar year and who is not a corporation. This form is to be filed by February 28 of the following year. The reporting of employee taxes is far more complex. If you have no one in-house who is up on these procedures, you might want to look into an outside payroll service.

The staffing process presents a real challenge. But the more practice you have, the better you'll get at it.

Marketing: The Crash Course

A "market" is defined in my dictionary as "a place where people go to buy or sell things." Marketing, by extension, is the act of offering goods or services for sale to people who are willing to part with money to get them.

When you first start your company, you probably won't have a very big marketing department. Probably there'll only be one person responsible for getting the word on your goods and services to the people who want to buy them. That person will be you. When your company starts to grow and prosper, it will make sense for you to bring on people to handle this part of the business. In the meantime, however, let's add a title to your resume: Chief Marketing Officer.

At Bancard, and before that at Tetra, I was the marketing department. I don't have a degree in marketing, but I have learned a thing or two about bringing products and services to the people who want them. One of the things I've learned is that it's a whole lot easier to market a "good" product than it is to market a "bad" product. A good product is one that satisfies the needs and wants of your intended, or target, audience and does so at a fair price. No amount of honest effort is going to convince the public to buy a bad product, at least not for long. Notice I said honest effort. There's a name for people who convince others to buy lousy products. They're called "con artists."

I'm not saying that an inexpensive product is a bad product. Wrigley's Doublemint gum and Hershey chocolate bars have been around for a hundred years with little variation. The market has decided that these are good products. And they're inexpensive.

I'm also not saying that an expensive product is, by definition, a good product. Do you remember the Apple Newton? No? You're not alone. Most people now working at Apple probably don't remember it either, or, if they do, they'd like to forget it. Does the name Iridium ring a bell? Guess what they spent to launch this network of satellite-based phones? Five billion dollars! And where is that company now? Nowhere. The key is to develop a good product and then, and only then, bring it to the people.

People commonly confuse marketing with sales and/or advertising. Sales and Advertising are a subset of marketing. They fall under promotion. They aren't the whole picture. True marketing starts long before you start knocking on doors or placing ads in the yellow pages.

People who study marketing refer to "The Five Ps." They don't always agree on what these are, but for our purposes we'll use these: **Product, Price, Positioning, Placement,** and **Promotion.**

Product: This is what it sounds like. Your job is to define and develop a product (or service) that satisfies a need or desire on the part of the public. This can be as simple as a better doorstop or as complicated as an entirely new technology. Our "product" at Bancard was an improved way for merchants to process their credit card transactions coupled with far better service than they had been receiving. Our "product" saved customers a whole lot of money and made their lives a whole lot easier.

Just because you think you need something, don't assume the public will want it or need it. One of the worst mistakes an entrepreneur can make is to misjudge the consumer's desire for a product. You may get a great idea for a new shower knob one day while you're in the shower. But before you mortgage your house and car, ask yourself, will other people want it? More importantly, will they be willing to pay for it?

Now that you've asked yourself these questions, ask other people. Ask as many people as you can, people whom you trust. Listen to their feedback. How can you make your product better? An honest "reality check" at this point can save you a lot of time and grief later on.

Price: Now that you've defined your product or service, how much should you charge for it? Should you just charge as much as you think you can squeeze out of the consumer? Probably not. Should you just pick a number out of a hat? Also, probably not.

Here's where market research and competitive analysis come in. I'm going to assume that you don't have the deep pockets required to hire a market research firm with a lot of ampersands in the name. How, then, do you find out what to charge for your product? Let your fingers do the walking. Get on the phone. Start talking to people. Find out what comparable products (or services) are selling for. Talk to the consumers who are using these comparable products. Do they feel as if they're getting a good deal? What would be too much to pay for the product? What would be so little to pay that it would make them concerned about the quality of your product?

Don't make the mistake of setting the price too low. This can be deadly, especially when you're first starting out. Many people assume that they can give away the store as a way of attracting new customers. What usually happens is that you set expectations in the minds of your customers and you can never raise your prices to cover your costs. There's an old joke that says, "We lose money on every transaction but we make it up on volume." Unfortunately, for many now-defunct dotcom companies, this wasn't a joke. It was a marketing strategy. "Cheap" is a negative. It implies poor quality and turns people off.

Positioning: Where does your product "fit" in the marketplace? Are you going after teens? Twenty somethings? Seniors? Is your product a luxury good or a consumer staple? Are you selling razors or razor blades? Before you can promote your good, you have to give some thought to the niche it will satisfy.

Placement: Okay, you've developed your product, you've priced it, and you've positioned it. What's next? You rush out and sell a ton of them and retire early to Tahiti. Right? Not so fast.

You have to consider placement. What will be the distribution channels for your product? Will you be selling it door-to-door? Will you sell it on the Internet? Do you plan on opening a retail outlet? Will you need distributors? How do you plan on transporting your goods to the market?

Do you plan on selling your goods through large chain stores? Have you considered the cost of shelf space in these stores? If you're talking about a service, will this service be performed at the customer's site or at your site?

What are the implications of selling through a middleman as opposed to dealing directly with the consumer? Have you considered their margins in your operating costs? Remember, nobody does anything for nothing. This lesson has been brought home to me since I started getting involved with book marketing and distribution. By the time all the middlemen take theirs, I guarantee you'll never get rich writing a book. Unless you're the next Tom Clancy, that is.

How will your choice of a distribution channel affect the size and structure of your company? Will you need to keep inventory on hand? Will you need a warehouse? How about a shipping department?

How will your choice of a distribution channel impact your promotional efforts? What impact will your distribution choices have on the media you use to advertise? Will you be able to piggyback off of a national chain? Will your promotional message be targeted to the end user, or are you really "selling" to the vendor? Remember, the vendor's primary concern is how profitable your product will be at retail. You need to understand your distribution channel in order to make these decisions.

It's a lot to consider. The alternative, I suppose, is just to "wing it" and figure things as you go along. This might work. I did it several times. Planning, however, could save you a lot of wrong turns and dead ends.

Promotion: This is the one you've all been waiting for. The big payoff.

At the outset of this section, I mentioned that most people think that Marketing is just Promotion. Now, you see that there's a lot more to it.

Promotion consists of all of the efforts you and your staff put in to let your target audience know about your product Promotion can mean anything from placing an ad in your local newspaper to developing a sales brochure. Promotion is what you do when you brag about your business to the person sitting in the seat next to you on the airplane or on the ski lift. (That's worked for me several times. Promote too much in inappropriate situations, and you could find your friends avoiding you.)

The major subsets of promotion are Advertising, Sales, and Public Relations. How you use each of these to promote your product depends on the type of product (or service) you're selling, the nature of your customers, and the demands of the marketplace.

Advertising is typically the way to go when your product doesn't require a lot of explanation. If you've only got thirty seconds to get your message across, you're not really going to be able to go too deeply into the features and advantages of your good or service. Advertising is also helpful as a way to get people in the door.

By contrast, face-to-face selling is key when your product *does* require some explaining. Imagine buying a house because you saw a commercial on late-night television. You're probably going to want someone to explain the particular facts and features of the home in question. Especially if you plan on living there.

Advertising and sales can work together. Think of how the major car makers market their products. They use advertising as a way to pique people's curiosity, to bring them into the showroom. If you watch a car commercial, you'll see that it's what the advertising folks call a "lifestyle ad." Typically, the announcer will be saying things like, "Blaze a new path," or "Set out for adventure." You usually won't hear about how much it's going to cost you or how much your insurance rates will go up. Once you're in the door of the dealer, the real arm-twisting can begin.

The third leg of the promotion milking stool is Public Relations. This can either be formal or informal. You probably won't be able to hire someone to write press releases about your company when you first start up. It might not ever make sense for you to have a public relations department. I never had one. But think about what it means to sponsor an event in your local community. This is public relations as well. Call up your local newspaper and offer to give an interview. Sponsor activities for your local high school. All of these activities fall under public relations. There's nothing wrong with getting your name out in the local community. Remember, these same folks will be your customers.

No matter how you do it, don't just assume that people (other than, possibly, bad guys) will come to you, beat your door down, and take whatever you've got. No matter how good your product or service is, you'll have to let people know about it. Spread the word. You are proud of it, aren't you? Even if you employ a large outside sales force to do the actual selling, an effective P.R. campaign can make their job much easier.

Sales and Sales Management

Let's take a few minutes for a further look at selling and at the employment and training of salespeople. As I've mentioned, this will be aimed primarily at companies whose sales are made away from the office. Much of what we cover, though, will apply to larger sales on-premises, and a number of the concepts can be used in retail-type sales. In these latter instances, a gum-chewing "Help you?" accompanied by a look of complete boredom and disinterest is encountered all too often and does not belong in a well-run establishment. Let's see if we can help you prospective retailers improve the level of service, also.

Our Sales Training Manual at Bancard was entitled, "Turkeys Work Harder Than Eagles." The idea behind it was that turkeys run around, flutter, make a lot of noise, and end up, where? On your Thanksgiving table. Eagles, on the other hand, are able to cover long distances with an apparent minimum of effort. How do they do this? They instinctively find thermal currents—rising columns of warm air that provide lift. In selling, which would you rather be, a turkey or an eagle? How do you go about finding and, when necessary, creating "sales thermals"?

I read about a man who described himself as "an Assistant Insurance Buyer." How do you think his formal job description really read? Take a minute and think about it. He "helped people buy insurance." So what he really did, of course, was sell insurance. Pretty clever, huh? I'm guessing that he was probably pretty good at it, too.

I've mentioned that you, the boss, need to be the head salesperson in your company. What's more, even if you don't do a lot of direct selling yourself, you very well may be hiring salespeople. The more you know about their job, the better you'll be at evaluating your employees' performance. And remember, salespeople, especially those who have been at it for some time, are a little different.

So let's get into it. You have a product or service that you think is valuable to someone. You've defined your market and you need to exchange your product or service for money. Hopefully, at a profit.

Okay, I'm the prospect. Why should I buy your product or service? You may have some ideas about why *you* like it, and these are valuable. But it's not your reasons that matter to me. I will buy your product *if and when I* decide that *I* need it or want it for *my* reasons, and not a moment before. There's no way I'm going to hand over my money just because you want me to. So what are my reasons? That's for me to know and for you to find out. Or, maybe, even *I* don't know what they are and you'll have to help me discover them. Remember the "Assistant Insurance Buyer"?

Where does that leave us? You can leave it to chance that I will take an instant liking to you and your product and insist on buying a whole lot of it. Or you can, like the Boy Scouts, "Be Prepared." How do you prepare? The same way knights of old did—you arm yourself!

"With what?" you ask. Well, perhaps your first weapon would be product knowledge. You need to know your product inside and out: its advantages, its shortcomings, its features, and most of all, the benefits it provides to the user. You also need to know your competitors' products equally well, especially their shortcomings and disadvantages. This does not mean, as we will demonstrate, that you will or should spew forth volumes of information on each sales call. No one likes to be drowned in a flood of speech. You've got to be prepared to answer pertinent questions. Obviously, you can't have all the answers, but you'd better have the important ones. You also want to avoid disparaging the competition. Keep it positive. Know their weaknesses and stress your contrasting strengths. There's a real temptation to put down your competition. You should resist that temptation. Think of the political ads you've seen that, instead of discussing the issues and what the candidate was going to do about them, used the time to talk nasty about the opposing candidate. Did that make you feel all warm and fuzzy about the person featured in the ad?

The second sword in your scabbard is sales materials. We are told that we absorb 50 percent of what we see, but only 20 percent of what we hear. Demonstrate, point out and, best of all, let the prospect get hands-on experience with your product, if at all possible. You will need to practice, practice, practice so that your demonstration goes as smoothly as possible. If it's appropriate, bring in a laptop and be prepared to give your prospective client a PowerPoint presentation. This will enable you to sit back and watch your prospect's reactions to various points and deal with these in the final steps.

Your final weapon, and this is the big one, is QUESTIONS. Lots of them. In a sales contest, the person who asks the most questions wins. Remember, we mentioned that you need to discover *my* reasons for buying? Well, folks, you uncover those reasons by using carefully phrased questions. We'll come back to this in a bit.

Many experienced sales trainers divide the sales process into five phases. Different trainers use different names for these phases, but these will do: **Preparing, Relating, Presenting, Summing Up, and Closing.** I'll add another: **Following-up**, and explain later how that ties into the process.

Step 1. Preparing

In addition to what we've covered earlier, this includes the nitty-gritties, such as:

Transportation: This is a requirement if the sale is to be made away from your place of business. Some sales can be made over the phone, in which case your fingers can do the walking. If you do use a vehicle, make certain it is presentable and in good mechanical condition. "Sorry I'm late, but my car broke down" is not the best way to start a sales call. If you take a prospect out to lunch or to visit another site, you don't want to have to apologize while you move the infant seat or clean trash off the seat. Make it a habit to arrive a few minutes early. Another good technique, especially if you'll be traveling a long distance to make the call, is to phone, either the night before or just before leaving, to confirm the time. This may prevent a wasted trip if your prospect can't see you for some reason. It also reminds him/her of the subject to be discussed.

Personal Appearance: The ill-fated Willie Loman, from *Death of a Salesman*, got by with "a smile and a shoeshine" for a long time. In these hi-tech days, that's not enough, but they're still a first step. You'll need neat hair, clean fingernails, appropriate clothes. Depending on the business climate where you do business, this might mean a suit, a sport coat, a dress, or slacks. It probably does not mean overalls or cutoffs and sneakers. If in doubt, go conservative. While you may be perfectly within your First Amendment rights to sport long hair, a beard, multiple earrings, or visible tattoos or piercings, give some thought as to the effect this might have on your prospects. Will this make your sales job easier or harder? I might enjoy looking at a cropped top and a pair of low-slung jeans but they certainly would impair my ability to concentrate on the sales presentation.

Sales Materials: You need these so that you can *show* and tell. They might include literature, samples, testimonials, references, charts, a PowerPoint presentation, a video tape, or some combination of the above. Be sure your materials are complete, organized, and neat. If you're missing a vital piece, fumbling to find something, or if you display a ragged, dirty product sheet, then you'll be walking up a steep hill. I've found a hand-held computer or laptop to be helpful for calculations, illustrations, etc.

A PowerPoint or taped presentation offers a couple of other benefits. In effect, the computer is acting as salesperson and you and your new buddy, the prospect, can sit together and watch it. Also, the computer doesn't forget key points. If you put them in, they'll still be there.

Knowledge of Your Prospect: The more you know about both the person and the company you'll be calling on, the easier it will be for you to relate your product or service to his/her/its needs. Time at the library, on the Net, or studying the company's advertising, etc., can pay off. You might want to pay an advance visit to look around and check out the place.

You may be familiar with the concept of Personality Styles. In any case, you will probably agree that people vary considerably in how they react and view life. The Personality Style concept classifies people into four groups, where a person's place is determined by how he or she interacts with others. If you can figure out which group your prospect falls in and you govern your conduct accordingly, you'll be better equipped to interact with him or her.

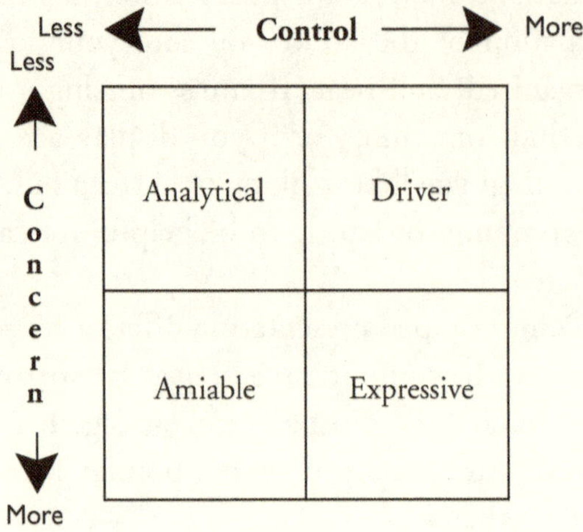

Look at the chart. The first thing you will want to do is estimate the degree to which your prospect wants to exercise **Control**, *in a business or negotiating situation.* Clues to this are whether he/she displays emotion in facial expression or voice tone, fails to make eye contact, sticks to the facts, uses specific language. After you have placed the person somewhere on the **Control** scale, try to determine where they fall on the **Concern** line. A more concerned person will speak slowly and softly, will ask questions rather than tell, will use the pronouns "you" or "yours" more often than "me" or "mine," will seldom interrupt, and will tend to lean backward.

Once you have determined how controlling and how concerned the person is, you can place him or her in one of the four boxes in the chart. Now you should have a better understanding of how to deal with this individual. Be aware that few people stay rigidly in one place along the scales and may very well move between styles in different situations. However, you want to determine where they are most frequently *during the sales process.* Now that you've determined what type of personality this person has, how do you deal with each of these personality styles?

First, **The Driver**—You can't tell him or sell him anything. He will tell *you* how it is and he will buy when *he's* good and ready. Give him the facts and he'll make the decision. Next, **The Expressive**—She's the life of the party, the person who gets up and sings and gets things moving. To get the job done with this type of person, you'll need to join the party and sing along with her. Third, **The Amiable**—On the surface, this appears to be the easiest to sell to. He wants to be liked. Be his friend and he'll buy from you. But, don't betray that friendship, or you will have made an enemy for life. Finally, the **Analytical**—This is probably the hardest to bring out of her shell and get the deal done. Again, the facts and figures, lots of them, but don't expect a quick sale. I have found few people more frustrating than those who sit quietly with their arms crossed, showing no reaction to what I'm trying to tell them. They want answers, so ask them questions to try to get a hint of what they're thinking. This could save a lot of time by pinpointing what you'll need to concentrate on. Patience on your part can do the trick. The good news is, once they've decided to go with you, it's just as hard for your competition to get them to change.

I need to caution you once more not to go off half-cocked with this concept. We've barely skimmed the surface of a complicated topic. My purpose here is to help you consider that people are different and you need to interact with them in a way that makes sense to *them*. Don't expect the same words and techniques to work equally well with everyone. Keep this in mind during every step of the sales process. Observe your prospect. From his/her words, tone of voice, and body language, try to judge what effect your words and actions are having. Are you making progress toward your goal or are you turning him/her off? Like a broken-field runner in football, be prepared to change direction as often as necessary.

Speaking of body language, as I've noted, you can often tell more from this than you can from words. Body language is another subject for a whole book. Pick one up, if you find it. We're not going to list all of the signals a person can send. However, some of the obvious signals are:

Body Language	*Signal Meaning*
Eyes Wide	Attentiveness
Eyes Narrowed	Suspicion
Leaning Forward	Attentiveness
Leaning Backward	Boredom, Withdrawal
Nodding Head	Agreement
Tapping Foot or Hand	Boredom
Looking Around the Room	Inattentiveness
Asking Questions	Interest

And the list goes on.

One of our sales trainers used to say, "Sell on Purpose." What he meant by that is you should always establish a goal for your sales call. That goal should be a vision of the prospect enjoying the benefits of your product or service, long after you've left. If you were trying to sell a car, for instance, you would want to create in your mind, and in the prospect's mind, a picture of him or her enjoying a pleasant drive in the country with the family. Feel the acceleration? Smell the leather of the seats? Anticipate the delicious meal at the restaurant up ahead? Get the picture? You want to make certain the prospect gets the picture, as well. On the other hand, if your goal (and the picture in your mind) is the $5 or $500 commission you hope to make on the sale, then that, too, will come through to the prospect. Remember, the prospect couldn't care less about *your* unpaid bills or the new car you have *your* eyes on.

The same trainer taught us to think, before we even started the sales process, about what we needed to get out of "the deal," and then put that out of our minds so that we could concentrate solely on the prospect.

And, finally: Know your product and your competitors' products inside and out.

Step 2. Relating

Consider your habits. When you get up in the morning, do you have to think about what side of the bed you'll use, which hand you'll brush your teeth with, whether you'll put on your right sock or your left sock first? When you drive to work, do you spend time thinking about which street you'll use? When you get there, do you consider alternative places to hang your coat? I suspect you do all of these things by habit, which saves you a lot of time and energy.

Habits can be useful or bad. Destructive habits might include smoking, excessive drinking, or failing to look carefully when proceeding through a stop sign. Other habits can be bad because they stifle progress, as in the "But we've always done it that way" syndrome. Habits, whether good and bad, are difficult to change. When you're asking a prospect to try your product, service, or system versus whatever he/she's been using, you're asking him/her to break a habit. The prospect is in the habit of using what's worked in the past. That's where the relating process can pay off. You would be more likely to accept advice or a suggestion from someone you knew, liked, and trusted than you would from a stranger, right?

Okay, let's say you've got a couple of minutes or a little longer to get your prospect to know you, like you, and trust you. Is this difficult? Maybe. Is it impossible? Heck, no.

Who is the most interesting person in the world to your prospect? Not you, that's for sure. Okay, who, then? Right, the most important person to the prospect is him/herself. Your job, at this point, is to get the prospect talking about him/herself and show that you both have common interests and feelings.

Before you went on the call, you did some research about the person and the company, didn't you? So you already know something about him/her. When you get there, look around. Try to find something unique about the company and the surroundings, something you think the buyer will be proud of. Continue your observation after entering the prospect's office. Does your prospect have a big fish hanging on the wall? Ask about it.

Ask some questions about the company, even if you already know the answers. Has it developed a new, unique product or service that has made the news? Has it had a long, successful history? Has it been a quick startup? Moved to a new location? Move on and ask some personal questions: Has your prospect had a long history with the company? Just been promoted? Made the news in some other way? Frame some more personal questions based on your observations. Have you spotted bowling trophies? Broncos/Raiders/Cowboys memorabilia? Family pictures? Pictures with celebrities? Military or civil awards?

I have a confession to make here. Spectator sports bore me silly. But you can bet that when I was actively selling, I knew the scores and trivia about the local teams and was prepared to discuss them when necessary.

The neat part is that you really don't have to be an expert on bowling/sports/local teams. Most times, just noticing and commenting on them will get your prospect talking, which is just what you want. You just have to nod, murmur, and, when necessary, comment. What're you doing here? Getting prospects to talk about their favorite subject, themselves, and relating, is the goal here. If you were trying to relate with me, for instance, what would be a good topic to talk or ask about? If you guessed "horses," you just guessed right.

Step 3. Presenting

At some point, if you're doing this right, you will sense your prospect start to relax and get comfortable with you. This is the time to begin your presentation.

Okay, you're full of product knowledge, you know all the features and benefits of your product, and you want to spill all of them out as fast as you can, right? Wrong! That approach is what one of our sales trainers used to call "show up and throw up." I finally refused to go out on calls with one of our people because he talked and talked and never gave the buyer a chance to buy. It drove me nuts.

So, if you shouldn't talk your prospect to death, what should you do? Here's where you pull out your most potent weapon, the real smart bomb. You ask **QUESTIONS**. Lots of them. What you want to determine is if and how your product fits the wants and needs of the buyer. Note the word "if." Should you determine at any point in the sales process that your prospect is really *not* a prospect, that he or she truly doesn't want or need what you're selling, save your time and his/her time and politely break off the conversation. You might ask him/her if there is someone else you might talk to who might want or need your product or service.

If you're still in the game, start to analyze the clues your prospect has given you. Use these clues to determine what features and benefits might be important to the prospect. Next, you want to reinforce these and find more. "Mr./Ms. Prospect, how would you like to save dollars (minutes, employees' time) in your manufacturing process?" "Suppose there were a system that would simplify your ____________? Would you like to hear about it?" "I'll bet you've worked hard to get where you are. If there were something that could get you out of here a few minutes earlier each day to spend more time with your family/your bowling league/at the lake, would you ____________?" "Do you agree that customer satisfaction is one of the most important parts of your business? Now, if there were a way to improve that, would you ___________?"

Take some time to put yourself in the customer's shoes, remembering what we've said about personality types. Try to think of some questions that might perk up your ears if you were the customer. Try them out and refine those that seem to work.

Once you've got a pretty good idea as to what turns your particular prospect on, zero in on those features and benefits and hit hard. Keep asking questions to test the effectiveness of your presentation. "Do you see where we're going, Mr./Ms. Prospect?" "Do you agree?" "Wouldn't that be nice?" "What would you expect your savings to be if we ________?" Keep him/her involved in the action. What you are aiming for are signs of agreement: nodding the head, pulling up closer to you, smiling, saying, "Yes, that would be nice."

If you get objections at this point, try to say something like, "Good question, I'll make a note of that and we'll deal with it shortly." You want, right now, to be asking the questions, not answering them. That'll come in the next step.

Step 4. Summing Up

First, summarize the main points of agreement, emphasizing the benefits, monetary and otherwise.

Then, turn it around and ask for questions. At this point you are inviting the dreaded *Objections*, every salesperson's nightmare! Nightmare? Not to us sales pros. In fact, if you don't get one or two, your prospect's probably been asleep during your presentation and isn't ready for the next step.

Be prepared to deal with objections. There are two types: genuine and B.S. Take the time to deal with the genuine ones. "Yes, but…" is not the right way to do this. Attempt to find a satisfactory solution to each problem and get his/her agreement that the solution is, indeed, satisfactory.

You will need, without offending the prospect, to show the B.S. objections for what they really are. Remember our talk earlier about habits? Let's say your prospect is in the (bad) habit of crossing a street without looking and one day he crosses into the path of a truck bearing down. Are you going to pay much attention to his objections when you push him out of the way? Keep reemphasizing the good points until he/she forgets about the garbage.

When you have covered all the points on the table, finish by asking if there are any other things that need to be clarified before you proceed to the next step. If there are, deal with them now.

Step 5. Closing

This is the part of the sales process most books and trainers seem to put the most emphasis on. They imply that this is the magic bullet, some kind of spell that you can weave on the client. On the contrary, I have found that, if you have done a good job on the previous four steps, the close comes easily and naturally. If you've blown it up to now, you can spend all day trying and failing to close the sale.

It may be that all you have to do to close is pull out your order blank and start writing. If the prospect doesn't stop you, keep writing. That's called the "Assumptive Close." I use this more often than not.

One of our sales trainers taught us "The $10,000 Close." He said he had had to pay someone that amount to learn it. It goes like this, and is probably worth memorizing verbatim:

"Now, you and I have come together today to find a solution to ________________. Is that correct? (Pause, and *say nothing* until you get a response.) In the past few minutes, we have agreed that the best solution is ________________, isn't that right? (Pause again until you get a response.) All right, in order to implement this solution and give you the benefits of

it, *as soon as possible,* <u>we</u> need to (sign this paper, put down a deposit, get your okay here, etc.), *for all the obvious reasons.*"

What are these "obvious reasons?" I don't know and you won't know, either, *but the prospect will.* He/she's not going to admit that he/she doesn't know them. You've just said they're obvious, haven't you?

Hand them the pen and *shut up*. Note the use of "you" and "we." It works. I've used it often. Make the $10,000 check out to Don Aspromonte, the sales trainer.

Other questions that have worked for me are, "How soon would you like ___________?" or, "Which do you prefer, the green one or the red one?".

Back when my sons were selling for my company, Steve, who at the time was nineteen, but looked about twelve, used his inexperience to his advantage. He'd get through with his pitch and the customer would say, "Okay, that all sounds great. When can you come back? "

He didn't know any better, so he'd say, "Never."

The customer would look at him in stunned disbelief and say, "What do you mean?"

He'd say, "It's nothing personal, but I do a lot of traveling and I honestly can't tell you when I can come back. I'd like to, but you know how it is. This is pretty much your only chance."

Often as not, the customer would sign up right on the spot. Now, this isn't the approach to take with everybody, but sometimes it works.

Here's a close I actually used sometimes, when I got the "Let me think about it" routine:

"Okay, Mr. /Ms. Customer, I'm leaving but, before I go, I just need to clarify something in my own mind. We agreed, *didn't we,* that using this service will save you, say, $100 a week; is that correct?"

The prospect nods.

"All right, and you'd like to think about it for how long? A week?"

"Yeah," Mr. Prospect says. "Give me a call in a week."

"Fine," I say. "I'm on my way. I'll call you a week from today. By the way, on my way out, I'm going to open your cash register and take out a hundred dollar bill. Is that okay?"

At this point, I would be in a half-risen position and I'd watch the prospect's expression. When he/she was about ready to explode, I would add, "Relax, I'm only kidding, but that's how much you're losing by not signing today. Shall I sit down and let's talk about this some more?" Sometimes I got thrown out. Other times I made the sale, then and there.

Step 6. Following Up

Many salespeople feel this is not part of their job, that it's the responsibility of others in the company. Some companies even encourage this attitude. These companies feel it might be dangerous to have their salespeople developing a close relationship with the customers and maybe taking them away some day.

I believe following up is an inherent part of the sales process. If you've played golf, try to picture the swing. You step up to the ball, look down the fairway, look at the ball, step back, maybe take a practice swing or two, step back up to the ball, take your back-swing, bring your club forward, hit the ball, and stop. Right? Of course not! What *do* you do? You follow through. Why? Because if you did stop your motion at the time of contact with the ball, your muscles would anticipate that and ruin your shot.

The same applies to selling. If the salesperson can't see beyond the close and cashing a check, it impedes the relationship with the buyer from beginning to end. As we've said, the salesperson needs to picture the customer enjoying the fruits of the purchase, with the salesperson standing ready to assist in any way possible. This sort of after-sale relationship conveys two benefits: the sale sticks, and the customer may refer additional sales. The salesperson needs to work very closely with the production and customer service people to help ensure that the promises made are promises kept. Remember the Ford Motor Company slogan: "Quality Is Job One"? We could add, "Customer Service Is Everyone's Job."

A few words about Sales Management

I've found, and you probably will also, that the best salesperson usually doesn't make the best sales manager. A couple of the traits that make a star salesperson are a strong sense of independence and, not infrequently, a very selfish nature. The best salespeople tend to be selfish, not only for themselves but also for their customers. They and their customers come first, no matter what. Good salespeople are not generally team players, certainly not in the long term.

If you're going to successfully manage salespeople, you need to understand what makes them tick, what turns them on. Money is usually a pretty good guess. The quickest way to turn them off is to screw with their pay. "Pay promptly and correctly, according to agreement" is probably Sales Manager's Rule Number One. Salespeople, because they are "doing a selling job" on their customers, are very quick to suspect that someone is doing one on them.

Although it may very well be necessary at times to alter a salesperson's terms of employment or pay schedule, try to plan ahead so that you can keep this to a minimum. There are a number of surefire ways to sow discord among the sales force: reduction of territory, reduction of commission or salary, adding additional duties—perhaps non-sales-related, capping their earnings. Think very carefully before doing any of these things. If you have to do one or more down the line, try to explain to your salespeople how the change will benefit both them and the company in the long run.

Contests and prizes can be a good idea or a bad one. Some salespeople are motivated by them. Some aren't. Recognition, though, is almost always good. We never went in for expensive trips, figuring that if trips were important to people, then they could work a little harder to earn more and pay for the trips themselves.

We did make a big deal out of our annual sales meeting. We would hold it at a resort in the Colorado Mountains or at one of the better hotels in town. The food and the accommodations were first class. We usually asked the salespeople to pay part of the expense of attending, on the theory that you place greater value on things that you have an investment in.

During the meetings, in addition to the motivational speakers, new product introductions, and teamwork lectures, we tried to get one of the movers and shakers in the industry to give a talk on "the big picture." We had games, usually with prizes, and tried to ensure that everyone, or almost everyone, could win something. One of our more successful ideas was to have the inside teams design and man booths where the salespeople could win "Bancard Bucks" by answering questions or doing tasks related to their jobs. Folks could then use the Bancard Bucks to bid on really good prizes at an auction held after dinner. One of the unexpected pluses of this was watching the big Bucks winners bid on prizes for others, often members of their support teams who had not been eligible to compete.

You will want to keep the sales force informed of anything that affects their jobs. This is a two-way street. We expected each of our salespeople to serve as our C.I.A. Part of their job was to find out and report anything that was new in the industry and, especially, new with the competition. We could then share this information with everybody. We made an effort to always have "the newest and the greatest" available for them to show to their customers. We also did our best to install team spirit. Each support team was linked to one or more sales divisions. We tried to emphasize to the salespeople how important "their" team was to their continued success. One unforeseen result of this was an occasional near-revolt in a sales division when one of their favorite support people was transferred or promoted out of the team.

The first page of each month's "Milking Stool" newsletter featured a ranking of the sales force by total volume and by new accounts signed that month. Because I had started first, I generally led the list in volume. It became a game among the superstars to "beat the boss." Each time that happened, I took the winner and his or her significant other to dinner at one of his or her better customer's restaurants. I made a big deal about his or her accomplishments. While a number of the troops, generally the less-motivated ones, didn't seem to care about climbing up the ladder, the better ones made an effort to "beat so-and-so" this month or the next month. It really ticked off our Number Two salesperson that she couldn't catch Number One, especially since Number One had been hired after her.

Most of the "middle 80 percent" continually tried to improve their place on the list. With the exception of the new kids on the block, the "bottom 20 percent" didn't seem to care. These were the ones slated for early retirement.

Mouse Traps, Again

In a retail business, production is typically a matter of purchasing, receiving, and displaying the goods. In a service business, production may involve generating ideas, rather than goods. We might define the general objective of a business as "producing the best possible product or service, considering the price, and delivering it to the customer as efficiently as possible."

Again, you will know (or learn) a whole lot more about the specifics of producing your particular product or service than I could possibly cover in this book. Try to remember, though, that your company is not solely about things. It's about people. Whether on the receiving dock, on the factory floor, in the stock room, or in the service trucks, *your people are your company.* If you can keep them involved and focused on the company goals and missions, if you can give them a feeling of ownership in their jobs and in what they produce, then you will come out all right. If, on the other hand, it's "us against them; labor vs. management,"—an attitude all too prevalent in many union shops—you'll have an ongoing problem.

Human Resources

A necessary but rather mundane side of human resources is record keeping. This will include initial hiring and ongoing evaluation and promotion records. It may also include payroll, either as a stand-alone function or in cooperation with accounting.

In this litigious age, I cannot overemphasize the importance of keeping complete and accurate personnel records. Document, document, and document. This is especially important when "counseling" and possible termination is involved. Keep records of all reviews, promotions, transfers, raises, injuries, absences, vacations. Document anything that affects individuals and their jobs.

Be certain that all personnel records are maintained under lock and key and that only authorized people have access to them.

Keep up on all federal, state, and local laws and regulations that affect employment and ensure that you and your company remain in compliance at all times. Particularly tricky and ready to bite are the following:

Fair Labor Standards Act – This basically requires that employees, with the exception of narrowly defined managers and certain others, must be paid overtime for working more than eight hours in a day or forty hours in a week.

Americans with Disabilities Act (ADA) – This legislation currently applies to companies with fifteen or more employees. It prohibits discrimination in hiring, promotion, etc., and requires employers to make "reasonable accommodation" for employees with disabilities.

Family and Medical Leave Act (FMLA) – This act currently applies to companies that have fifty or more workers at any one site. Affected companies must allow a worker to take an unpaid leave of absence in connection with the birth or an adoption of a child, or for a serious health condition involving either the employee or a close family member. Some states—California, for instance—have even more stringent laws on the books.

A few more land mines

Something you want to avoid at all costs is sexual harassment. If an employee can prove that your workplace is "hostile," then your company may be liable for both actual and punitive damages. And, finally, step carefully in a termination case to try to avoid being charged with unjustified termination. As I've documented elsewhere in this book, this is something I can speak about from personal experience. It can get very expensive.

We've only touched on this subject. Please consult with an attorney early on for guidance and keep yourself up to date on possible changes and additions to the various regulations. It's up to you to be informed.

Whether you are your own H.R. person or you delegate the function to someone else, it is important that your people feel that they have an accessible, disinterested place to turn to for help with personal, preferably job-related, problems. Counting on supervisors and coworkers may work, up to a point.

Sometimes, though, whether for privacy reasons or because the problem is a little more complex, more specialized resources are required. Again, let me emphasize that the H.R. person, you or someone else, needs to know his or her own limitations. The person in charge of H.R. needs to know when to get involved, when to stay out of it, and when to make a referral to a lawyer or a mental health or other professional. Be a little cautious in your recommendations, however, or you may find yourself sharing liability for the other person's failure to solve the problem satisfactorily. Check out each resource on your referral list and encourage the employee to seek out alternatives.

Customer Service

I think we can agree that it does little good to sell lots of things and have them come back as fast as they go out. We have already talked about Quality Control of product and people. Now we have to put them both together with a focus on our ultimate boss—the customer.

Who's in charge of Customer Service? Get out the mirror again. It's up to you to constantly show, by word and deed, that the customer really *is* the person in the middle of the circle and that the company revolves around him or her. If you do this, your people will get the message. Likewise, if you perform and tolerate sloppy customer service, then your people will get *that* message.

I have come to the conclusion that most businesses, especially the larger ones, just don't get it. I think most CEOs are aware of the direct relationship between customer service and customer retention. Somehow, that message gets lost on the way down the pipe to the folks who actually deal with the customers.

When I got back in the bankcard business, I signed back up with a large Dallas processor because my friend Nancy was a V.P. there. I had confidence that, should a problem arise, all I had to do was call Nancy and she would kick butt and take names. She never let me down.

Unfortunately, Nancy has since moved on to other places. It took me awhile to "train" the other people there so that I no longer hear when they are faced with anything slightly out of the ordinary, "That's not my job," or something similar. At Bancard, if one of our people had that attitude, he or she received "counseling." If this didn't get the point across, he or she found himself or herself back on the job market.

I depend on these people to support my efforts to service our mutual customers. When they don't, it makes my job harder.

Here's another example of sub-par service: When my customers need supplies, rather than stocking them, I utilize companies that drop-ship for me. To help prevent errors, I fax the orders. Recently, a customer complained about receiving the wrong item. I had to make three calls to get the right thing shipped and the incorrect shipment picked up. When I received credit for the returned merchandise, the person responsible for the error included a note that "the customer had ordered wrong." Blaming the customer does nothing to avoid the reoccurrence of the problem and has a negative effect on future business. I'll be using another source from here on.

We have a local radio personality in Denver named Tom Martino. He is now syndicated nationally and you might be able to catch him in your local market. He calls himself "The Troubleshooter." For three hours each weekday afternoon (in the Denver area), he takes calls from people, generally complaints about one business or another. In the majority of cases, he finds that the caller is correct, and he really takes off after the business involved. He will often call the owner of the business on the air. He doesn't hesitate to use names like "sleazebag" and "slimeball." Believe me; you don't need that kind of publicity. Although he does take the business's side when he thinks they are right, you probably don't want Mr. Martino calling you. You especially don't want to be listed on his website (www.troubleshooter.com) as a member of his "Sleaze Brigade." Perhaps if the businesses listed took Customer Service more to heart, they could keep off the list and keep more of their customers.

Another watchdog organization is the Better Business Bureau. Its local affiliates take complaints and give the business a chance to tell its side and remedy the matter, if appropriate. They log each complaint and its disposition and make the results available to future callers. Hint: Join your local BBB. It's not expensive, and I have to believe they will work more closely with a supporting member when a complaint does arise.

Let's talk a little more about how to avoid negative attention. Try as you may, you won't please everyone, especially on the first go-around. "Zero Defects" is a nice goal to have, but it's probably not attainable over time. Also, "misunderstandings" will arise between your sales force and your customers. Sometimes they are just that. Other times they are result of the salesperson' being what we'll call "over eager." Would a salesperson lie?

The best solution to problems is to prevent them in the first place. Continually educate your production and sales teams so that they do it right the first time. Establish checks and balances to prevent errors and to allow you to produce and market the best possible product or service.

When the inevitable problem does arise, have systems in place for fixing it quickly and correctly. Follow up with the customer to ensure that the matter was resolved to his or her satisfaction.

Here's an example of *good* customer service from the side of the customer. I buy promotional items from a company called National Pen. When I received an order of calendars, I realized that I had forgotten to order envelopes for them. When I called, feeling like an idiot, to order the envelopes, the customer service person put me on hold for a minute and then came back to say, "I've found some envelopes. I'm shipping them to you at no charge." Will I remain a customer? Guess. They haven't paid me for an ad, but their website is www.nationalpen.com.

If you follow these suggestions, you'll find that life—for you, your employees, and your customers—becomes a whole lot more pleasant.

Accounting 2.0

Whether or not you are handling this function yourself, you will want to continually monitor the system to make certain the records are accurate and current.

Are your Accounts Receivable under control? Are bills being paid promptly to maintain your credit standing and take any available discounts? Are there any payments to people or vendors you don't recognize? Is payroll being handled correctly? Are your taxes being paid as due? Are *you* being paid on time?

You should have access to the books at all times, preferably on your own computer. This will enable you to keep an eye on things at your convenience, without anyone knowing when you're doing it.

Make certain you are receiving and are familiar with the necessary reports. I find long columns of figures boring, and if I don't discipline myself, tend to jump quickly to the bottom line. In the final years at Bancard, we were lucky enough to have a competent, hard-working CFO. Since it was his buck as well as mine, you can bet he went over the books with a fine-toothed comb. He instituted procedures, such as outsourcing a number of functions, that turned the company into a cash cow. I stood in awe at how the quarterly distributions had increased.

There is more to accounting than just keeping the books. A good "numbers person" can be a real asset to the company.

Sources of Additional Capital to Maintain Growth

Remember my sailor brother's maxim: ***The faster the ship moves, the more fuel it consumes***? The same applies to a business. If it takes X dollars to get from A to B, then it'll take X-plus dollars to get from B to C.

The object of the game is to generate sufficient profit to cover X-plus and still be able to make reasonable distributions to the owners. If your growth is outrunning your capital, however, you may need to turn again to sources of outside funding. These are pretty much the same sources we covered in Chapter One: family, friends, banks, venture capitalists, and the public.

If you can show a successful track record to this point, then your job will be much easier. Brush off your marketing plan and update it. You should be able to slim the wording and concentrate on your numbers, both past and projected. If you can show a steady, impressive growth in both revenue and income and demonstrate how you'll maintain the trend, then you should be able to raise the necessary additional capital without mortgaging the farm.

You have the same decision to make that you made at the beginning: borrowed funds or equity? If you believe you will be able to repay the amount in a reasonably short time, then borrowing might be your best option. At this point you should be able to find a much more receptive audience at your bank. They know you, they can see your track record, and they can better evaluate the degree of risk involved.

If, on the other hand, results to date have been less than spectacular, your task may be even harder than it was at the beginning. Lenders and investors have heard it before: "All we need is one big break." If you really believe this and you're not kidding yourself, then go out and sell the idea. However, if, in your heart, you have big doubts about the future of the company, now may be the time to think about winding it up.

Maybe you can structure a sale of the company or its assets, possibly to a competitor. It may be better to salvage something now rather than wait for the final crash.

A couple from Iowa had been good customers at High Country Trails, the riding outfit I used to run with my partners, the cowboys. These folks had returned several times to ride with us. On their final ride, I confessed that we were running out of funds and would need to shut down the outfit. They offered to invest to the tune of several thousand dollars, which was big money to us then.

After they left, I thought about it and thought about it and finally decided that they would just be throwing good money after bad. My wife overheard my phone conversation with them to break the news and was furious with me. "Quitter!" she hollered, "I've put heart and soul into this business, cooking meals and answering the phone, and now you're going to chuck it!" In my best John Wayne drawl, all I could think of to say was, "Yep." Then I ducked.

It broke my heart to sell off most of the horses I'd babied for two years, but it had to be done. It was time to go back to the real world and a real business. Some things work out better than others.

Chapter Four

What Have I Done?—The Maturing Business

Going from "My Company" to "Our Company"

One theory holds that people who are skilled at starting a business fall by the wayside when the business is up and running. According to this theory, most entrepreneurs lack the managerial and housekeeping skills needed to shepherd along a maturing company. Steve Jobs, of Apple, seems to disprove this. He co-founded Apple, left for a while, then came back to run things. The "other Steve" (Wosniak), on the other hand, seemed content not to return. Bill Gates, although he has given up the title of CEO, is still very much involved in minding his not-inconsiderable stake in Microsoft.

As the business grows and changes, the people running it must grow and change with it, as well. Now that considerable money and other people's livelihoods are involved, it might not be appropriate to take the risks that were acceptable, necessary even, during the start-up period. At this point, you're no longer making decisions for you alone.

A verse in Kipling's poem "If -" reads:

If you can make one heap of all your winnings,
And risk it on one turn of pitch and toss,
And stoop, and start again at your beginnings,
And never breathe a word about your loss -
- Then you'll be truly adult and mature.

If that happened to me, you'd hear me crying from here to Moscow. You'll find the whole poem, by the way, in the Appendix. I think it makes a pretty good guide for life as well as for business.

There are numerous stories about folks who have made millions, lost millions, and then made them again. Bully for them. But how, I wonder, did their seesaw fortunes affect their associates, their employees, their families?

I managed to grow one company for fourteen years and another for nineteen, but I will admit to having had anxious moments along the way.

I took no business management courses in college. I don't think Harvard offered any at the undergraduate level. I did take a basic accounting course there, for which I'm grateful. Later, I took a very good accounting correspondence course. I've never been employed in a senior management position at a large company. If I had, it might have helped me to make the transition from running a small company to running a not-so-small one. As it was, I pretty well had to play it by ear. That worked okay for me, up to a point. Perhaps I should have taken advantage of one of the postgraduate executive courses offered by the various business schools, such as Harvard or Northwestern, but I never seemed to have the time. You might consider attending one of these courses at some point in your career.

There are also a number of so-called "boardroom" programs offered by various companies. For a fee (a pretty large one) they consult with business owners to try to help with problems they are encountering. They meet for lunch once a month. Over lunch a moderator leads a group of executives of supposedly non-competing companies in a discussion.

I'm sure some or all of these programs are effective, but, boy, are they expensive! I went to an introductory breakfast given by one such organization. Everything went fine until someone asked the price, which was several thousand dollars a year. The guy sitting next to me asked, in a whisper, "Why don't we try to set up something like this ourselves?" So we did. We ended up with probably a dozen local small-company owners. We met once a month in Bancard's conference room and threw out problems and suggestions. We were able to attract some pretty good guest speakers, including a professor from the University of Colorado Business School. What was the cost? The price of a sandwich or pizza. Would the boardroom company's sessions have been more effective? Certainly they would have been more structured. But we did okay by ourselves. This is something for you to think about. You get similar benefits for nowhere near the cost of the commercial operations.

Another thought would be a real board of directors. Not your brother-in-law, unless he can really contribute something. Probably not your banker, lawyer, or accountant, either. What you would be looking for as a board member would be someone whose business skills and experience complement yours. You also want someone who is not afraid to ask questions and will tell you when he or she thinks you're off base. You don't want someone as an outside director who is on the payroll, directly or indirectly, or who has a vested interest in sucking up to management. (I first wrote this several years ago. As I revise this edition, it has become the hot topic in the financial pages.)

When the day-to-day details start to get you down, it may be time to consider hiring a chief operating officer, or the equivalent. You can let him/her handle the day-to-day operations while you concentrate on ideas.

My thing, in case you haven't guessed, is sales. It always was, always will be. Aside from my time in the Air Force, I've held only one job that wasn't sales related. And I hated that job. The only thing that kept me there for two years was the quarterly twenty-five-cent-an-hour raises that kept coming. When those stopped, due to a recession, I was outta there. As soon as I could, at both Tetra and Bancard, I found someone else to take over the nitty-gritty so that I could concentrate on sales. Jim and Connie, my successors at Tetra, preferred running the inside of the business, so they have had a succession of sales managers.

What's the point of this? At the beginning, you might have been able to say, along with the narrator in W. S. Gilbert's poem:

"Oh, I am a cook and a captain bold,
And the mate of the Nancy brig,
And a bo'sun tight, and a midshipmite,
And the crew of the captain's gig."

In case you stopped to wonder how the gentleman quoted could have had so many jobs aboard ship, it had been shipwrecked and he had eaten the rest of the crew. (From *The Yarn of the Nancy Bell*, one of my favorite poems from grade school).

What I'm saying here is that you might, at the beginning, have been able to handle everything yourself. But after a while, as the company grows, you want to be able to concentrate on what you do best and hire someone (or find a partner) to do the other stuff. One of the good things about growing is that you have the resources to start delegating.

While it may still be "your company," be aware that other people, your associates and employees, now share an emotional ownership, at least to their little part of the company. Or, rather, they should, if you have done your job right. You should be hearing words like "my department," "my cubicle," "my project." Encourage this. Welcome and share this type of ownership and consider it when making decisions and changes. Change can be hard on everyone, even you.

As I've said before, try to discourage the Not Invented Here (NIH) syndrome. Encourage new ideas, from whatever source:

customers, employees, vendors. (Hey, another use for The Milking Stool!) Evaluate each idea and adopt the good ones. But, make sure everyone involved buys in to the greatest extent possible. Major changes may take time and preparation.

The key is to **plan ahead** so that as the company grows, you don't end up, as the saying goes, herding cats.

Another Look at the Market—Has It Changed?

Boy, they really gobbled up your product in the past, but what about now? Probably the three most powerful words in marketing are "**New!**" "**Better!**" and "**Free!**" (Whenever I hear "**Free!**" I get a good hold on my wallet). Have you kept evolving your product to stay ahead of your competition? Have you kept up with the changing tastes of your customers?

Surprising as it may seem, there really is a market today for buggy whips (I own several), but I suspect the demand for them is much less than it was one hundred years ago.

One of my favorite companies, Microsoft, exhibits sheer genius in staying one or several steps ahead of the competition. They are masters at the **Newer! Better!** game, without having to actually use the words. Windows 95, when it came out, was a giant step forward. It enabled Microsoft to close the perceived gap between its operating system and Apple's. Just as people began to see the flaws in that Windows version, presto! Windows 98 was introduced with the attendant hype and hoopla. Fast forward to Windows 2000, Windows XP, and whatever's in the works. Just when you're beginning to see through the smoke, it's **Newer! Improved! Better!** With each successive version Microsoft is able to add copy protection and tie the market ever tighter to its other products and services. And we get to pay them for this. Genius!

Keep in Touch with Your People

As your company has grown and matured, the structure, both formal and informal, has evolved. You probably no longer holler out your office door, "Bessie (or Jimmy), get me the file I was working on!"

Do you still know the first (and last) names of all of your people? Do you know the names of their spouses and children? What's the new procedure for getting a letter out? For handling a customer problem? For deciding on a new piece of equipment?

Each time a new person started in our office at Bancard, I made it a point, during my walk-around tours of the office, to stop by his or her work station, address him or her by name, and ask how things were going. I made notes of this individual's answers and discussed them, where appropriate, with his or her supervisor. Whenever I could, I would ask of both new and old people, "Got any ideas for doing the job better?" Ask, and ye shall receive.

Although, in later days, other people had the authority to sign company checks in my absence, I tried to adjust my schedule to be in town for bi-weekly check-signing. First, this helped to give me an idea of where our money was going. I would ask for backup on unusual expenditures and question the controller on any I didn't understand.

Equally important, I developed the habit of writing notes on the stubs of paychecks, congratulating the recipients on any particular accomplishments during the period. A number of the troops later told me that they had looked forward to getting these pay stubs and had saved them.

Since many of us still live in or around Boulder, and since I am back in the credit card business, I frequently encounter Bancard "alumni" in various places. Judging by their comments, our system was effective.

One of the things I found difficult in a larger company was the feeling that I was getting "out of touch" with the front line troops and with the customers. Gone were the days when I was *the* night crew, answering the business phones at my house after five. On the other hand, I really didn't miss being awakened at one in the morning by a hotel night auditor. As the company grew, we ran three shifts, giving real 24/7 service. But I missed the feeling that I knew all the customers and could solve all of their problems myself.

As it grows, the real way the company functions is completely outside the parameters of the operations manual. Your people, on their own, will develop ways of getting things done—shortcuts. Some of these are good; some may be not so good. You may not be aware of all of these shortcuts. It's good to have a confidante among the troops who keeps you informed of the "real" situation. By this, I don't mean a spy. The object is not to "get" anyone. The object is to make sure you are informed about how things really work.

Often, the informal way proves to be better than the formal way. In this case, thought should be given to incorporating it into the company's regular policies and procedures. During World War II, the Boeing Company maintained what they called "The Skunk Works." With minimal direction and interference from upper management, this group solved many problems and came up with some of Boeing's most profitable innovations. Some of our best ideas came from front-line troops. After all, they knew their own jobs better than anyone else. We adopted the better ideas and made sure the author was recognized, whether with an extra bonus, a gift certificate at a local store, or a dinner for two on the company.

I made certain we avoided the pitfall of "We never did it that way." I never wanted to hear this used as a reason for not trying something new. Obviously, some of the "great new ideas" did not work out, but no one was ever punished for trying.

One of the inevitable aspects of an informal structure is, unfortunately, the rumor mill. Rumors can be very counterproductive. Try as you may to keep everyone informed, rumors will start and flourish. Often, they'll develop a life of their own. It pays to encourage everyone in the company, especially your confidante, to come to you with the rumors, so that you can take action either to confirm or to refute them.

As your work force expands, you will need to intensify your efforts to keep everyone on the same page. You'll have to work harder to make certain that, as far as humanly possible, the troops' objectives remain in line with the company's. This will ensure that the company remains a win-win situation for all.

Systems: There's Always Room for Improvement

As the company grows, many of your procedures will become more formalized. There will be fewer actions taken off-the-cuff. As with most things, this can be good or bad. When there were two or three of you, you might get together for coffee in the morning and say, "Let's try this. If it doesn't work, we can always pitch it and go back to the way we did it before." When you're dealing with dozens or, perhaps, hundreds of people, this isn't so easy. Before making major changes, you will need to consider their effect on the folks down the line. Communicating the intended changes and re-training the people involved can be expensive and time consuming.

This doesn't mean, however, that your procedures should be set in stone. As we've said before, there's always a better way to do something. One of the primary functions of you and your managers (actually, of everyone in the company) will be to find those better ways and determine if they are, indeed, better.

Here, again, watch out for "It's not my job." If your people are properly trained and motivated, then they'll agree that "it," whatever "it" is, is everybody's job. At one of our local restaurants, when a customer's order is ready and his or her waitperson is serving another table, someone else picks up the order and serves it. That's the kind of attitude you want to encourage at your shop.

You also can mine those "better" ideas from your customer base. And your sales force can help you do it. They and your front-line support troops will constantly hear suggestions and complaints from your customers. Ignore these at your peril. A really unhappy customer often won't even bother to complain. He or she will just take his or her business somewhere else.

Be proactive in this regard. I used to periodically pick the names of a dozen or so customers, call them and ask, "What are we doing right? What could we improve? Is there anything we're not doing that you would like us to do?" Some of the requests, of course, will prove impractical or impossible. Other requests will have you saying, "Hey, why didn't we think of that?". If you do adopt an idea received from a customer, then be sure to let him or her know. In this case, a small gift or a dinner out would be appropriate and reinforce the idea that your company is his or her company.

When you decide to implement a new idea, especially a major change, you may not want initially to disrupt the whole company. Instead, you might set up your own informal "skunk works." Try the idea out in one department. If it works, then expand it to other departments. If it doesn't work, you haven't bet the farm on it.

Acknowledge the ideas that you receive, both good and bad, and reward the originators of the good ones. For your customers, a dinner for two might work wonders.

It's always good to let your customers know that you're thinking of them and appreciate them. I'm not sure that Christmas cards are effective for this purpose. One "out of the box" way I did this was to print labels for all my personal customers prior to going on vacation. I'm a riding nut, so I've taken several riding tour vacations in some pretty out-of-the-way spots, like Argentina, Kenya, Turkey, and Italy. Each of my key customers got a hand-written postcard from each of these places. I would get a kick out of seeing these cards on their walls when I visited later. It was worth the effort to write and stamp a couple of hundred cards.

Early on, I instituted the practice of referral awards. Each time we signed a new customer referred by a present one, the referrer received a note and a check. We started with $25. Presently, it's $100.

However you do it, make sure you take the time to acknowledge those folks who are taking the time to make your business work.

Benefits

If you haven't done so already, now might be a good time to set up an employee benefit program. This is a good recruiting tool and morale booster. Also, you can generally get more bang for the buck by adding benefits than you could by increasing salaries, since your company gets tax breaks on benefits.

Health insurance, whether completely paid by the company or offered on a premium-sharing basis, is almost a must, as soon as you can afford it. Having a sick or injured employee with no insurance coverage is not something you want to deal with.

As most of us have trouble maintaining a regular savings program, you might want to establish a 401-k or similar plan. Think twice, with Enron in mind, about including company stock in any plan. Also, pick your plan administrator with care. Some are a lot better than others.

I've always had mixed feelings about participating, myself, in one of the government-mandated plans. What Uncle Sam giveth, he also taketh away. The thing that has kept me out is the thought of eventually paying taxes at the full rate on what were capital gains. This is a personal choice. When people at work asked me about my retirement plan, I answered, "You're standing in it." Many people need automatic payroll deductions to ensure that they put something away.

We also paid tuition for selected employees. For selfish reasons, as well as to comply with government regulations, courses for which we paid had to be related to the employee's present or future positions with us. We included a provision that if the employee left before a certain time, then a portion of company-paid tuition had to be repaid.

Expansion

Okay, you've built a good shop and, through your marketing and sales efforts, demand is exceeding your ability to produce your product(s). Or you're taking care of the customers locally, but you want to establish another location to serve a customer base in a different city, state, or even country. Let's think big. What's the first thing you need to consider? Renting a store, office, or factory? Negotiating with the local government to get the best tax breaks? Nah.

Assuming you've done your homework and the additional location really will be a plus for your company, the first thing you need to consider is...surprise! PEOPLE. Who will run the new facility? Will it be one of your present key people? A new partner? A new managerial hire? What qualifies this person for the job? Why would he/she want it? What's in it for him/her? How will the two of you communicate on a regular basis? How will the new manager be incented to produce the results you expect? How will you manage communications and control? How will you train new people?

As you have come to expect by now, I have a story from my past that illustrates how *not* to do it.

About a year before I moved to Colorado, I attended a weeklong class at Wilson Learning Systems in Minneapolis. The course was called Counselor Selling—Leader Training. Northwestern Mutual Insurance was using the course and I had an opportunity to sit in on one of their sessions. I was impressed. I wanted our sales force to attend the Counselor Selling classes. I had a choice of paying one of the Wilson people to give the course or taking the Leader Training class and teaching it myself. As you would expect, I chose the less-expensive latter route and took the instructors' class. Not only did it save money, but I also have found that the best way to learn something is to have to teach it. I made the right choice. I learned the material very well.

What didn't work so well were the classes I taught, even aided by Wilson's manuals, leader guides, and visuals. We had a pretty wise-ass, full-of-themselves bunch of salespeople. They came into Chicago on successive Saturdays, and the first sessions went okay, although I got no job offers to join Wilson as one of their instructors. During the last Saturday session, I lost it. I can't remember the exact problem but, somehow, they really got to me, and I started stammering and getting red in the face. Very fortunately, two of the local Wilson trainers had decided to sit in on that class and one of them stood up and took over. Within a few minutes he had the group subdued and the session back on track. He impressed me so much that, when I knew I would be leaving Chicago, I offered him the job of sales manager, which he accepted.

You've already heard the rest of this story. As a sales trainer, he was the best. As a sales manager, he was a complete bust. He sure knew the talk. He wasn't so good at the walk. He took up his time and the salespeople's time with long, detailed, and irrelevant reports. In addition, his relations with the operations folks deteriorated to the point where I was spending too much time on the plane back to Chicago to referee fights. This interfered with my enjoyment of the Colorado experience and my attempt to expand the Mountain States' sales territory. More to the point, had the situation continued, the company was heading straight for the dump.

Here's another "how-not-to" story: We found a restaurant in Boulder that quickly became our favorite. Naturally, in the course of one dinner, I asked the owner if he would like to improve his credit card system. He did, I did, and we became friends. As often happens during an installation of a new credit card system in a restaurant, I spent considerable time in the kitchen, training the wait staff and making sure everything got off on the right track. I helped mop floors, too.

During these sessions, I became increasingly impressed with the way the place was run. The kitchen was immaculate, the systems were in place, and the staff functioned like the proverbial well-oiled machine.

All went well until our friend left for Vail to open another place. He left an affable, well-liked maitre d' in charge. The Boulder place, which had been packed most every night, folded in less than six months. When the cat's away....

Large multinational companies have elaborate hiring and staff-development programs in place, and even they screw up when it comes to developing people. I have been known to observe that large companies can make large mistakes, but small companies had better limit their errors to small ones. Otherwise, they cease to exist.

So that you don't get too depressed, here's a story about expansion, with a few twists and turns but a happy ending:

As Bancard started doing well in the Boulder/Denver area, we decided to expand our sales force, with a view toward going national. Among our first efforts were ads in the various entrepreneur-focused magazines. These didn't bring the results we had hoped for. Generally, the people who answered these ads were looking to make a lot of money without working too hard. If I knew how to do that, I could sell the secret for a whole lot of money, myself.

I'm a strong believer in word-of-mouth. I slipped gentle hints to salespeople with other companies who appeared promising, especially to those working in related industries, such as check guarantee. This produced some winners. As we grew and "The Bancard Story" spread around the burgeoning industry, we began to attract salespeople from competitors who hadn't figured out The Milking Stool concept.

One of my friends and former competitors was the first in our group to sell out. The sales price was a reputed $7 million. I had never known anyone worth that much! My friend put me on to his former sales manager in New Jersey. This gentleman, whom we'll call Paul, turned out to be both a curse and a blessing. Paul was bright, capable, and hard working. Unfortunately, his philosophy was "Me first, and screw you." He had a problem with the truth and hired others in his mold. Paul and some of his hires got us into a number of awkward situations. I'd have customers telling me, "But the salesperson *promised* [the moon, a lottery win, etc.]." Paul solved our problem by resigning just as we were figuring how to fire him.

The blessing was that Paul jolted us out of the "we're doing alright" mode we were in at the time and got us hustling again. He also, perhaps inadvertently, hired some good people, one of whom became our best salesperson *and* our best divisional sales manager. This person, Joan, just tore up the territory. At the time I left, she was earning over $300,000 a year in commissions and overrides! Her husband, who helped her out and had his own accounts, was doing pretty well for himself, as well. Part of the arrangement when we eventually sold the company was stock options that we could distribute to selected employees. You can bet that we took good care of Joan and her husband.

By and large, with a little luck, we ended up with good people in all of our divisional manager slots. They, in turn, found some capable regional managers to work under them, and so on, down to the sales reps.

What was the secret of this success? These folks bought into our story and soon saw that working both hard *and* smart would benefit them as it benefited the company. Most of them didn't need a lot of guidance from me. After their initial training session, they figured it out and went into overdrive.

On the other hand, anywhere from three to fifteen people would attend each of our monthly training sessions for new salespeople. From their response, or lack of it, over the three-day session, I could pretty well predict which of them would last their first year with us.

You'll note that I used the word "luck" earlier. In your expansion plans, you don't want to depend too much on luck. I've heard it said that people make their own luck. I would tend to modestly agree with that sentiment.

Looking into the Future

Okay, it's now ten years down the pike. This might be a good time to pull out your original business plan and review the section on "Where will I want to be ten years from now?" Are you there yet?

I'm not going to ask, "Are you having fun yet?" That's a given. What's changed? Have the changes been good or bad? A little of both?

Now might be a good time to revise the plan. Where do you want to be ten years from *now*? What are you going to do about it? Are you working on expansion plans that will help you get to your next goal, or are you content to coast at your present size? I firmly believe that businesses either go forward or backward; they don't stand still.

Are you considering an entirely new business? I did, as you'll remember. Depending on your age, are you considering retirement? If you really like what you've been doing, then retirement sucks. Take it from me.

Legal Matters, Continued—When the Best-Laid Plans Go to Pot

I hate to put this in here when I've got you all whipped up about success in your business. Sometimes, however, things go the other way, and you need to know various options for bailing out. I have, unfortunately, had to deal with several. Before you give up, though, there are a number of sources for help, depending on what the problem is. The SBA again comes to mind. Their SCORE (Service Corps of Retired Executives) may be able to suggest solutions to your problems. There are consultants of all stripes, some probably better than others. Friends or acquaintances might have solutions to offer. Suppliers, customers, or even competitors might be willing to lend a helping hand. Maybe your lawyer, accountant, or banker has an idea. There may come a time, however, when throwing in the towel is the sensible thing to do.

How do you know when it's time to throw in the towel? Here are a few signs:

You haven't enough cash on hand to meet the next payroll.

Looking down the road, you can see that your revenue just won't cover all of your expenses.

You've misjudged your market and the demand for your product or service just isn't there.

Your differences with your partners have reached the point where you don't sleep at night.

Okay, you want out. What to do? Selling the business or the assets is an obvious first thought. What might you have that someone else wants? Obviously, if you're deep in the stuff, you probably won't get a very good price for the business, but something should be better than nothing. Magazines, when they stop publishing, often find their subscriber lists can be valuable to another publication.

Just closing up is another option—lock the door and take off. I'm hoping at this point that you've listened to your lawyer and me and have structured your business so that you aren't personally liable for its debts. Before you do this, consider the effect on your Milking Stool components—your customers, your suppliers, and your employees. What do you owe them, and not just in monetary terms? Also, you might talk to your attorney to review any consequences of this action.

The United States Bankruptcy Code provides two different paths for dealing with an untenable business debt situation. **Chapter 7** deals with liquidation of the business. In brief, all the company's assets, under court supervision, are divided among the creditors and the company ceases operation. **Chapter 11**, on the other hand, allows the company to reorganize, eases the pressure of debts incurred prior to the filing, and allows the company and its creditors to try and work out a plan satisfactory to all sides. Under this plan the creditors would agree to partial payment of what is owed them. The company then can continue to function. You can operate under Chapter 11 protection for several months, which may give you and your creditors time to work out things and give you a fresh start.

For further information, check the Internet under "Bankruptcy Code" and consult with an attorney specializing in this aspect of the law.

I won't get into further details, but I've had occasion to become more familiar with this subject than I cared to be. If it should happen to you, rest assured that you're not alone.

CHAPTER FIVE

All Good Things Must Come to an End

Will You Die with Your Boots On?

Successful companies usually outlive their founders. What will become of your company when you want out or go out?

What you *don't* want is to get hit by a car before you have made any plans for succession. You don't want to leave both your family *and* your company scrambling to adjust for your sudden absence.

You might decide to hand the reins to a (presumably younger) partner or other top manager. Large companies start grooming the next CEO years in advance. You'll want to make sure that whomever you choose to succeed you will be up to the task.

Then there's the thorny issue of ownership. Will you feel comfortable having a large part of your wealth and your family's inheritance tied up in a company that's being run by someone else, no matter how close this person is to you? You should consider this matter well in advance. When I bought into Tetra, the seller's contract stipulated that he would run the company until I acquired the whole operation. That worked out well, as he had much to teach me. After the final payment, we extended his contract as president for an additional year.

Often an all-cash buyout is impractical, especially for a company that has grown substantially. Thought may need to be given to financing arrangements.

Many companies, large and small, have passed successfully from parent to child to grandchild and so on. These range from household names like Ford and DuPont to companies with names like John Doe & Son. I spent two of my high school summers sorting wool fleeces straight from the sheep at my grandfather's company, S. Silberman & Sons. That company lasted for three generations of the same family, a statistic that beat the odds.

Discussing company matters around the dinner table can have either a positive or negative effect on your offspring. Some begin to see heading the company as their destiny. Others are completely turned off and can't wait to embark on something entirely different. Worse yet, some youngsters do go into the family business and make a mess of it.

My son Steve, at age four or so, used to amuse the crew at Tetra when he would sit in my chair and proclaim, "When I run this company...." During his freshman year at Harvard, after he and the university mutually decided he needed a year or so off, he jumped in his car and began peddling bankcard processing around the country.

On a trip to Aspen, Steve signed up a storeowner who had said, "No kid is gonna sell me anything." The owner was so impressed that he asked to join the company as one of our salespeople and gave up the store. Steve's commissions made during that year helped to pay for his books and living expenses at school. He went back and finished Harvard in three years and still occasionally goes out and signs an account for our new company, PRO PAY. His real interest, though, is writing, and that's how he makes his living.

My son Jack, at a later age, began selling for Bancard and worked his way up to the position of divisional manager. He was eased out along with his father, shortly after the sale, and did not have the opportunity to advance further. He is currently selling for PRO PAY and may very well take over one of these days.

My daughter Gillian's interests lay in an entirely different direction. She and her husband recently concluded a successful stint of property management in Chicago and have moved to Oregon to try their hand at organic farming. There's no harm in determining your youngsters' interest in working at and, possibly, eventually managing your company. They will find, however, that having the same last name as the boss is more of a curse than a blessing, especially in the early days. In order to earn the respect of coworkers and subordinates, they'll have to prove themselves at every step of the way and work twice as hard as their peers. Each time they stumble or merit recognition, someone'll be heard mumbling, "Whaddya expect from the boss's kid?"

You will need to resist holding your child/employee back for appearance's sake. You also don't want to promote your children before they are qualified to take the next step. Just as having the "same name" is a problem for the youngster, it will cause you many a sleepless night. Your other shared problem will be keeping parent/child attitudes out of the workplace. At work, your children need to be talked to and treated just like any worker in their comparable situation. Likewise, you won't want to have shoptalk dominate the dinner table conversation, especially if other family members are not involved with the company.

The reward, of course, is seeing your offspring take the company on to greater heights.

Actual ownership, in dollars and cents, is a cause for concern also. Would you be happy having your fortune in the hands of one or more of your children? Will you count on dividends or distributions to finance your retirement? Even if your future daily bread is assured, transfer of the company will have major tax consequences. Doing this without careful thought, planning, and a little "creative accounting" can result in having an unanticipated additional partner, the IRS. Discuss transfer of ownership with your trusted accountant well in advance.

Selling Out

Now you're on the other side of the transaction we discussed earlier. You're the one who's selling the business. The situation is entirely different. It's your baby, you know it's worth a ton, and someone out there is going to try to steal it for peanuts.

If you prefer easing out over a period of time or lightening your administrative burden, you might consider sale of only a part of the business, i.e., taking on a new partner(s). This would be similar to your having taken on a partner at the formation of the business. However, you will have accumulated a lot of experience and sophistication along the way that will help alleviate some of the uncertainty involved in the relationship.

You'll have to think about sharing control. You have been running things pretty much on your own to this point. Now you're going to have to share some of that authority with your new associate(s). Usually, unless the by-laws or other governing documents state otherwise, a person or persons holding an interest greater than 50 percent of the company can pretty much call the shots. Minority owners, though, have certain legal rights that should be respected, unless you want to find yourself in court. Again, avoid a 50/50 ownership at all costs. This could greatly complicate important decisions.

If you have been the sole decision-maker for some time, then you probably would not be happy giving up a majority interest. In this case, you will need to find one or more people who will be satisfied to let you retain control. You might consider, as we did in the Tetra purchase, an initial partial buyout with either an option or a requirement to purchase the balance of the company at some future date.

One of our neighbors in Colorado ran a small business that performed the arcane function of "metal cladding." This process involved bonding a thin sheet of an expensive metal, such as titanium, to a thicker sheet of a more common material, such as steel, for reinforcement. For some reason, his company never seemed to be able to make a profit. He was forced to sell off ever-increasing portions of the company to raise the necessary funds to continue operations.

One day, the other investors, who by then held a majority of the shares, met and ousted our friend from his CEO position and completely out of the company. You probably don't want that to happen to you.

Depending upon the size of your company, a sale can be a quick, simple transaction or an intensely complicated one. One thing you want to try to do, during the sales process, is to keep your emotional attachment out of it, to the greatest extent possible. Obviously, you want to realize the greatest possible gain, but you owe something to the eventual buyer. You don't want to be gloating, Midas-like, over your bags of money while the other guy is cursing you for cheating him. You also will want to consider the effect of a sale on your people. They've helped to get you to this point. What do you owe them?

Perhaps a logical first step would be to have the company evaluated by an independent outsider. If possible, this should be a person familiar with your industry. I would suggest you not use anyone who might benefit in some way from the sale of the business. A person with a financial interest may be tempted to over-value the company at first to sign you to a listing contract and then under-value it later to make a quick commission.

The very large companies employ "investment bankers," Wall Street types who make a bundle doing just this. Jack Welch, in his book, had good things and bad things to say about these people. When we were just starting the process of putting Bancard into play, we were approached by a number of these large firms. Boy, were they slick talkers! They almost had us convinced that we would get ripped off if we didn't sign with them before taking another step.

Luckily, Tony Sdao, my partner and VP of Operations, was a quick study. He listened to the pitches and figured that it wasn't rocket science. And, besides, we knew our industry and its players a whole lot better than the Wall Street boys. Tony went ahead and prepared what is called "a book," a document that gives interested buyers the facts they want to know. We then put the word out to our associate banks and large competitors and waited for the storm. It came, and they came. It was comical to hear some of them tell us that if we didn't sell out to them at their price (and right now), we were doomed. My favorite of this bunch was a guy from Texas. His company owned a small bankcard company in Boulder, one that had never made a profit. He talked and danced the Texas Two Step, trying to figure out how he was going to maintain control when our two companies were merged. Somehow, he never got around to mentioning the magic word: CASH. One major processor flew their team into town on the company jet. They knew I was into flying, so they offered to let me fly in the jet if we made a deal. I pushed my luck and asked if I could fly in the co-pilot's seat. The answer was, "No way, Jay!"

After we heard them all out, we accepted the best offer, all things considered, and pocketed listed shares, eventually worth about $60,000,000. Not too shabby. See, I told you this story had a happy ending.

The earlier sale of Tetra, a much smaller company, was concluded in one morning with a handshake. Connie, Jim, and

I all knew what the business was worth and there was no negotiating. We just needed to let the accountant and the lawyer draw up the papers.

Unless you have a Connie and Jim, or a Tony, you probably will need professional help when it comes time to sell the business. Unless your business has remained very small, I would suggest that you don't need a "business broker." To my knowledge, these are actually real estate salespeople who hold themselves out to have some expertise in the selling of businesses. I'm sure there are good ones, but I have never met one. Ask yourself if you really want a real estate person determining the value of your hard work up to this point?

If you *are* going to sell the business yourself, be prepared for some humbling experience. Buyers, even legitimate ones, are going to doubt everything you say and pry into places you didn't know were there. Be prepared to bare your soul and everything else, but before you do that, have your attorney draw up a confidentiality agreement and make each visitor sign it. Be aware that this gives you only limited protection. Competitors with little or no intention of going through with the sale will welcome the chance to snoop around and gain a competitive advantage.

If the deal is big enough to warrant the use of an investment banker, then make sure that you understand what is involved. Before they sign a contract with you, they will probably give you a rough estimate of what they think your business will bring. They will expect a healthy percentage of the selling price, *plus expenses*, and they go first class on a client's money, whether or not they make the sale.

The actual selling process is very much like selling anything else. The difference is you will have a much bigger emotional and financial stake in this transaction. You have a product and you need to find someone who needs or wants your product bad enough so that they'll pay your price. How do you determine their needs and credibility? You do it the same as when you were selling your other products: you pre-qualify and ask questions. If the potential buyer is in your same industry, this will simplify the process. You and the potential buyer already know something about one another and share a common language. If, on the other hand, the buyer is an individual or company with little or no knowledge of your business, you will need to educate them. Before you start telling them anything, you do what? You ask, that's right. "Mr. or Ms. Prospect, what interests you about this business? Why do you think it would be right for you? What do you know about our industry? What do you know about other companies in the industry? Would you be running the business yourself from the outset, or will you want to retain or bring in experienced management? Will you be combining it with other businesses in the same or other industries?" And so on. One of the things you want to discover, in your own subtle way, is how the buyer will pay for it. Will they be paying cash or financing it? If the deal will be financed, will you be expected to carry the debt? Will it involve a stock swap? If the other company's stock is not listed on an exchange, how will you determine the value of its stock?

Knowing as much as possible about the potential buyer early in the process will help both of you determine if the fit is right and will facilitate the negotiations.

Hopefully, you will be able to agree on the major details, such as price, before you need to bring in the accountants and lawyers. These folks are sometimes called "deal breakers." If you and the buyer both know where you are going and have agreed on the essentials, then you can let the specialists concentrate on the details. As always, remember that they are advisors, not decision-makers. Heed their advice, the advice you're paying for by the hour, but make your own decisions. Remember, when it comes down to it, it's not their company and it's not their money.

Going Public

A third option to consider is taking your company public. I've not experienced this, so this section will be a short one. I'll just give you a few reasons for going that route and the reasons we decided not to. If you're considering going public, you will certainly want to consult with qualified people.

Reasons to go public:

1. To provide a potential source of additional capital to expand the business
2. To achieve broader public recognition
3. The ability to have employees as shareholders
4. To diversify your assets by allowing you to sell a portion of your ownership to the public

Our reasoning for not choosing to go public:

1. The process itself is long, complicated, and very expensive
2. We did not want to have the Securities and Exchange Commission (S.E.C.) and other government agencies overseeing everything we did
3. We really didn't want outside shareholders concerned with what we did and didn't do
4. We weren't interested in pressure to make each quarter look good, at the possible expense of long-term goals

If you do go public, will you, personally, want to continue in the spotlight? Some owners relish their newfound notoriety. Others shrink from the unwavering gaze of their shareholders and the public.

This is a decision you will need to make on your own. Obviously, not going public has been the right route for many.

What's Next for You?

Assuming you are no longer associated with what was your business, you will need to determine what to do with the rest of your life. Should you retire? Start over? Work with one or more community service organizations? I've done all three in the past few years. I can give you some insights.

When we closed the deal on Bancard, I had a one-year management contract, and a reasonable belief that I would be working there for some time. We had been assured, during the sales process, that we had the best company in the industry and there would be no changes after the sale.

About a day and a half after the deal closed, things began to change. I became increasingly unhappy with the new working conditions. To be fair, I was probably not a model employee after thirty-odd years as a head honcho. Things finally came to a boil nine months later when it was "suggested" that I collect my paycheck for the remaining term of the contract and go home. I learned since that this is not an uncommon occurrence in takeovers and mergers.

I have to tell you, friends, not getting up and going to work after all those years was a jolt. I am well aware that probably the majority of workers in this country are counting the days until that magic retirement day. When you've been part of building something and you looked forward each day to new challenges, however, being suddenly sidelined just doesn't cut it.

For some years, I had been associated with a couple of nonprofit, horse-related (what else?) associations. I suddenly had time to become more active in their day-to-day functioning. Also, I had started a new company that rented executive suites. I was a partner in the company that was constructing the building and the adjacent retail space. I became involved, with a friend and ex-competitor, in the vacation rental business in Tennessee. I started writing this book.

None of this really took the place of going to the office, interacting with the troops, calling on customers, and solving their problems. I spent a pretty restless year. Judy commented, on occasion, that she married me for better or worse, but not for lunch.

Just about a year later, two things happened at about the same time. One of my former Bancard customers called me at home. She said that they had become increasingly displeased with Bancard's service after I left and had switched to another company. The new service turned out to be even worse. Would I consider getting back in the business? Almost simultaneously, I received a letter from the company who acquired the company that bought us. The letter canceled my employment agreement, which just happened to include a non-compete clause. I was now free to get back in the business.

I made a couple of calls to friends in the business, and PRO PAY was born. Will it become *Bancard, the Sequel?* Probably not, at least not through my efforts. Like it or not, at seventy, we are not the same person we were twenty years ago. The energy to knock on doors and baby-sit a high-maintenance sales force just isn't there. Besides, it would interfere with my standing Wednesday riding date.

At this point, PRO PAY gives me just what I want—an expanding but still relatively small customer base and contact with an industry I have grown to love.

As I write this, we are at the point where we have to decide whether and how we are going to continue to grow. We are getting to be a little too much for one person to manage, but hiring an assistant would put a real dent in the net income. I'll wrestle with this for a while and then probably dump it in someone else's lap.

Would starting a new business work for you? Why not? You did it before and you can do it again. In this fast-changing world, new opportunities are constantly cropping up. The advantage you have now is that you have years of experience behind you. Also, you have a much better idea of what works and what doesn't. Who knows? Maybe you can write a book.

Here's a caveat: Don't be too sure of your own infallibility. Don't assume that because you were a whopping success in one business that you can easily duplicate your triumph in another one. One of my friends who sold his credit card business put the proceeds into a start-up satellite TV operation. He managed to lose his shirt. Whether his timing was off, or his faith in his fellow man was misplaced, the new business didn't work, big time. Don't bet the farm at this stage, unless you can afford to lose the farm. To quote the rest of Shakespeare's advice through Polonius:

And to thine own self be true,
For it must follow, as the night the day,
Thou can'st not then be false to any other man.

As I mentioned, you can become involved in charitable work. Community service organizations range from the huge (the Red Cross, the Boy and Girl Scouts, the American Cancer Society) to the small (the community church, a neighborhood food bank, animal care facilities). The large ones have elaborate organizations with extensive facilities and a large professional staff. The smaller ones are generally dependent on a group of more or less dedicated volunteers with, perhaps, one or two paid staff members.

Perhaps you have been active in one or more of these prior to retirement, but you now have more time to give. What route will best serve your interests and the interests of the organization? Should you be an active volunteer? An advisor? A board member? An officer? Perhaps you might consider a position on the staff. You will need to explore the opportunities and then make your own decision.

One more caveat. Larger charitable organizations operate like businesses. Most of the smaller ones don't. These organizations may be run very differently from the way your profit-making business was run.

I was a volunteer board member of a small non-profit organization. Dealing with these folks on an ongoing basis was one of the most frustrating experiences I have ever had. These were people with the best of intentions. They were very much involved with the purpose of the organization. Their hearts were in the right place. Unfortunately, with one or two exceptions, none of them had the least experience in how businesses are run. They thought and made decisions with their hearts and not their minds.

I know that the larger and, probably, some of the better-run smaller charities can attract well-prepared board members who can make good decisions. But beware. The skills and attitudes that made you a successful entrepreneur may or may not be suited to the non-profit world. Probably the best of the smaller groups are fortunate enough to have effective leadership. The Humane Society of Boulder County has a person like this. Jan McHugh Smith, the organization's CEO, had she so chosen, could have been very successful in her own business. Luckily for the dogs, cats, rabbits, and other animals in her care, she decided otherwise.

Jan, with the help of her super-competent staff and dedicated volunteers, completed financing and building a new $4.5 million facility, all in the space of two years, from concept to move-in.

I don't want to discourage you from community service. We all owe it to our country and our local area to give back to the society that provided such an opportunity to us. Just be aware that non-profits may be run very differently from how you ran your company, and be prepared to deal with this.

So, Are There Any Questions?

Okay, there you have it, a conception-to-retirement companion for starting, running, and, maybe, selling your very own business.

Can I guarantee that you'll be successful? No way. Only you can make that happen. But I hope that I've mentioned some things here that will make it easier for you. If you benefit from my experiences, both the good and the bad, then reading this book will have been worthwhile.

All I know is that if you're the type of person, like me, who needs to start and run a business, then it's the only way you're ever going to be happy. I've never been able to swing it for long as a mate on someone else's ship. Some people make great employees. I am not one of those people. Probably, if you've made it this far in the book, you aren't either.

For my money, there's nothing to equal the satisfaction of watching your business and the people involved in it grow, develop and prosper.

If you have questions or comments on anything in this book, you can e-mail me at jwhearst@msn.com. I will do my best to answer all e-mails.

I wish you all the best of luck! It's not going to be easy but it will be rewarding. Keep your courage up and stay focused and you'll be able to "LEAD THE CHARGE TO BUSINESS SUCCESS!"

APPENDIX

I

Aphorisims

Mine and Other People's

You may want to paste some of these on your computer monitor. Or you may not.

If you're going to lead, **lead**. From the front. - JH

Lead, follow, or get out of the way. - Anon.

Unless you're the lead dog in a sled team, the view along the journey is pretty much the same. – Anon.

There are three ways to succeed in business - You can ride the wave, create your own wave, or swim like hell. They all work.
- JH

The buck stops here. – Harry Truman

A turtle never makes progress when its neck isn't out. – Anon.

Wise men learn by other men's mistakes, fools by their own.
– H. G. Wells

When the going gets tough, the boss starts selling. - JH

A leader may do this, or may do that, but will always do *something*. - JH

"Keep on jangling" and "Don't look back. Something may be catching up to you." – Satchell Paige

That was then and now is now. - JH

Nothing happens in business until somebody sells something.
– Anon.

It costs a whole lot less to keep a customer than it does to get a new one. – Anon.

II

"If-"

Rudyard Kipling wrote this poem in the late 1890s. It has been one of my favorite poems since childhood. Gender issues aside, it is an excellent guide for running a business—and for living a life. "If" you will read it and consider it, line by line, it will make a whole lot of sense.

IF-

by Rudyard Kipling

If you can keep your head when all about you
Are losing theirs and blaming it on you,
If you can trust yourself when all men doubt you
But make allowance for their doubting too,
If you can wait and not be tired by waiting,
Or being lied about, don't deal in lies,
Or being hated, don't give way to hating,
And yet don't look too good, nor talk too wise:
If you can dream—and not make dreams your master,
If you can think—and not make thoughts your aim;
If you can meet with Triumph and Disaster
And treat those two impostors just the same;
If you can bear to hear the truth you've spoken
Twisted by knaves to make a trap for fools,

Or watch the things you gave your life to, broken,
And stoop and build 'em up with worn-out tools:
If you can make one heap of all your winnings
And risk it all on one turn of pitch-and-toss,
And lose, and start again at your beginnings
And never breathe a word about your loss;
If you can force your heart and nerve and sinew
To serve your turn long after they are gone,
And so hold on when there is nothing in you
Except the Will which says to them: "Hold on!"
If you can talk with crowds and keep your virtue,
Or walk with kings—nor lose the common touch,
If neither foes nor loving friends can hurt you;
If all men count with you, but none too much,
If you can fill the unforgiving minute
With sixty seconds' worth of distance run,
Yours is the Earth and everything that's in it,
And—which is more—you'll be a Man, my son!

III

Sample Business Plan

NOTE: A friend of mine who is now running a successful business prepared this. Lacking one of my own, I have included it merely as an example. As I've noted previously, your plan must be *your* plan.

COMPANY BUSINESS PLAN

Contents

CONFIDENTIALITY STATEMENT

The information and data presented in this summary are strictly confidential and are supplied with the understanding that they will be held confidentially and not disclosed to third parties without the prior written consent of COMPANY.

EXECUTIVE SUMMARY

Company Name:
Formation Contact:
Address:
Telephone:

PROPOSED BUSINESS DESCRIPTION

______________ (COMPANY) seeks to operate as an Independent Sales Organization (ISO) whose function is to develop a traditional merchant services business. Our low-cost operations, 7 years experience in the merchant services business coupled with 15 years experience in developing and training large, successful independent sales forces, along with a strong and proven personalized customer service program will allow COMPANY to grow dramatically in the coming years.

CURRENT POSITION AND FUTURE OUTLOOK

COMPANY is a new company formed by two existing companies: COMPANY 2, a 15-year-old marketing company and COMPANY 3, a 7-year-old merchant services company. From initiation, the 2-year, 3-stage program will consist of 1) developing the local Atlanta, Georgia, small to mid-sized markets, along with the development of a sales-agent training program; 2) development of a local, and ultimately, a national sales force of independent agents with exponential growth of merchant accounts; and 3) development of large corporate and non-profit accounts. Our long-term goals will consist (if possible) of the development of International and large Internet business accounts.

INITIAL STAFFING, SETUP AND COSTS

With over 22 combined years of experience, two corporations will pool their talents, equipment, programs and low-cost systems to develop QCP. Their operations will be initiated in a home-office environment consisting of over 1,200 sq. ft. of space in an existing 6,500 sq. ft. home in a secured subdivision. All office equipment—including numerous computers, desks, training materials and media equipment, large-scale copying machine, fax, and phones—is already owned by the principals. They will start the business by moving approximately 350 accounts. All initial expenses and fees will be paid through this income. Any additional expenses, if any, will be paid for by the principals.

___, owners of Company 1, a 15-yr.-old company, have had extraordinary success in building both national and international sales organizations. One such sales force of independent contractors (they developed from scratch) achieved $50 million in annual revenue in their third year of business with products averaging a cost of $130. Many of their top sales people have earned millions of dollars. These individuals and many others will be contacted to produce similar results with QCP.

______ has been the one involved primarily in recruiting, training and motivating their sales forces. __, with 3 different companies, have achieved a top 5 ranking in sales, recruiting, revenue production and training. Among hundreds of his peers, ___ has been chosen as trainer of the year for two successive years. He has also worked as a motivational speaker all over the world, speaking to audiences of up to 12,000 people. In his most recent position with an Internet company, he developed a direct sales force of 3,000 people to market Internet services nationwide. He tripled the sales revenue from $300,000 in 1998 to $1 million in 1999.

____ has had a very successful career with the _____ Corporation and brings top administrative experience to QCP. Her positions with _____have included Branch Controller, Branch Manager, Customer Service Manager, Order Entry Manager, Field Service Manager, Customer Rep. Training Manager, and Public Relations Training Manager.

_____ has had 25 successful years of sales experience and more importantly, 7 years in the merchant services business. _____'s background includes bringing International companies to the U.S. marketplace and introducing them to major retail stores such as ____. In 2 years, ___ developed a market of over $15 million dollars of sales for ______. Regarding the merchant services business, _______ was head of sales management of Financial, a large processing company. In addition, ___ served as training director and Equipment Deployment Coordinator. During the 1996 Olympics, _____'s company installed 37 ATM machines and established over 350 accounts in 90 days. ____ has established over 1,000 accounts personally over the last 3 years.

SERVICE UNIQUENESS

In today's market, personalized service is a must for long-term customer and business relationships. The establishment of local agents will be trained not only to develop new customers but also to do so with a level of quality service that will maintain those customers over a long period of time. We will not hire existing sales agents who do not commit to working under our strict standards. The purpose of QCP is to develop a long-term business that focuses not only on the development of new customers but also to retain them by developing a high–quality, personal-service program.

Most "brick and mortar" businesses are not equipped for or relevant to exclusive Internet business operations. These companies do most of their business person to person. Thus, we will develop our business "under the radar" of high-tech and establish a solid and large volume of merchants with high retention, thereby giving us a constant income stream as we develop new dimensions to our business. ____'s expertise in customer service as well as ____'s retention success in his merchant services company will be essential in the development of a training program for our sales agents to duplicate the existing success.

STRUCTURE AND OPERATIONS

- COMPANY will be jointly and equally owned by ____
- A Board of Directors has been established with equal representation. We have also received calls from friends and business associates who run or own large companies. Some have expressed future interest to be on the Board. Among them ___, owner of___, a large real estate conglomerate in Atlanta (presently building $75 million worth of real estate and managing well over $100 million worth of property she has already successfully built).
- Sales, recruiting and training will be managed and developed ___
- Office operations will be managed by ___
- COMPANY initial staffing will only include the four principals. Any additional staffing will not be necessary until the development of a sales force that exceeds the present capabilities of ____. We believe that additional help will occur when we exceed around 200 contracts per month.

VISION AND MISSION STATEMENT

COMPANY seeks to develop a long-term viable company in excess of 30,000 customers and 180 highly trained and qualified sales agents. Our mission is to provide complete satisfaction to our customers by delivering the highest degree of service, efficiency and quality in the industry.

OBJECTIVES AND STRATEGIES

Our objective is to become one of the largest and respected ISOs in the merchant processing business. We plan to develop our business in the following way: 1) acclimating ourselves to the basics of the industry by developing personal sales in the Atlanta marketplace; 2) through experience, perfect our training program and begin hiring a few sales agents; 3) once the hiring and training process is perfected, then hire a larger sales force to develop the metropolitan Atlanta market; 4) expand to the major cities of the southeast, the first of 6 regions; 5) once perfected by means of training competent managers, we will then focus on developing the final 5 regions, opening office centers in each region; 6) as we grow larger and more efficient, we will begin to approach national chains and franchises. Steps one and two are already in process. By the time we consummate an agreement with a processing company, we will be prepared to implement step 3.

PRODUCTS AND SERVICES

Due to our 7 years in the merchant processing business, COMPANY has developed relationships with numerous companies that now give us access to virtually all of the equipment required by almost any business. We plan to be a one-stop shop for the needs of each customer we service from terminals, check guarantee, PIN pads, debit cards, and mobile units to ATMs and check-cashing services.

PRICING AND VALUE

Our prices for products are extremely low and allow for competitive pricing as well as profit. We have an entire program in place with product providers who not only sell us new and used equipment but service our products as well. Part of our value is a merchant service package that will ensure the customer that our equipment will last for the full term of the lease, as well as some additional proprietary features that will eliminate concerns that many merchants have with their day-to-day operations. This program has been instrumental in maintaining a high retention rate for customers.

MARKET RESEARCH AND ASSUMPTIONS

Last year, over 2 million businesses were formed in the United States. The percentage of those needing processing equipment is very high. In Atlanta alone, the metropolitan area is projected to grow by over 2 million people by the year 2010. The number of new businesses in most of our metropolitan counties exceeds 2,000 businesses a month. With over 10 counties surrounding Atlanta and experiencing exponential growth, the local area is ripe with new business. Many cities across the Southern portion of the United States are experiencing the same kind of growth. Thus, we plan to expand primarily in the south and the west. Our assumption is that new businesses will not see a dramatic shift in growth over the next few years at least. In addition, we believe that our reputation and sales force will reach out to existing companies and obtain their accounts as well. This opens the market to millions of businesses throughout the United States. We are planning to provide a generous compensation program for our agents who switch customers (with integrity) to COMPANY.

MARKETING STRATEGIES

As mentioned, our customer profile will be primarily small brick–and-mortar businesses. We will not do business with Internet companies, due to the high risk associated with them as well as the impersonal conditions associated with them. As we progress and grow, we will approach larger companies that can be handled by our company and sales agents, regionally as well as nationally.

Regarding competition, our experience over 7 years suggests that price, though important, is not the singular item of concern. We have had a number of accounts leave us that returned to us as soon as they fulfilled the new contract they signed. The primary reason for getting our accounts back is due to the extraordinary service they received prior to changing their account. Efficient and quality service will differentiate us in the marketplace, along with competitive pricing and a high degree of professionalism. Such practices will lead to larger and more challenging accounts.

CONCLUSION

COMPANY is truly positioned for tremendous growth. We have been contacted by numerous highly successful independent sales agents. (Some have earned over $1 million dollars in commissions in a year.) All of these individuals have worked with us in the past. We have just reached an agreement with a 30-year-old company that we have had a close relationship with for 14 years. They will be sending us potentially 200–300 new high-quality accounts per month. This, we believe, is only the beginning. Our administrative and sales staff have deep experience in running successful ventures with independent sales forces, as well as working with large Fortune 500 companies.

FINANCIAL SUMMARY

ESTIMATES*

TOTALS	2000	2001	2002	2003
======	====	====	====	====
POS Devices Active	85	2,440	5,440	8,100
Trans/Device/Mo (75)	6,750	871,500	3M	6M
Avg./per Trans ($50)	$337,000	$43.5M	$150M	$300M
Number of Active Agents	4	80	90	100
Large Corp. Accounts $1-5 Million per yr.	0	12	18	24

*Personal contacts with owners of large corporate accounts with over $50,000,000 per year in sales each and with over $1 billion dollars per year in total sales have not been included.

IV

Sample Employee Handbook

This handbook is similar to the one we developed for Bancard. It is in use at a company with which I am currently associated. Feel free to adapt it for your own use, but I would advise running it by someone who is familiar with current labor law in your locality. We paid a lot of money for it; you may have it for free.

EMPLOYEE HANDBOOK

INFORMATION CONTAINED IN THIS HANDBOOK IS CONFIDENTIAL

If given a copy, you will be asked to return this handbook should your employment with the company terminate. Reproduction of this handbook in any form is prohibited.

IMPORTANT NOTICE

ALL EMPLOYEES ARE EMPLOYEES-AT-WILL, unless you have a written contract that specifically states otherwise. This means that you are free to resign at any time for any reason, and the company is free to terminate the employment relationship at any time for any reason.

This handbook is designated to give guidance to full-time employees, but there are many sections that apply to anyone performing work for the company.

VERBAL PROMISE

The Corporate Officers and General Manager are the only individuals authorized to make any agreements that would alter any information contained in this handbook. The agreement must be in writing to be valid. Any changes or agreements must be agreed upon by the General Manager and at least one of the Officers. Verbal promises will not be honored by the General Manager without the appropriate paperwork.

INTRODUCING THE ____________________, LLC.

The ________________, LLC was opened in the summer of 1999. Our intent is to provide entrepreneurs, expanding companies, sales teams, agents, and successful businesses with a great way to grow and expand their businesses.

Executive suites have been around for quite some time. Struggling entrepreneurs looking to keep their overhead low by sharing space and resources developed the original idea. By allowing profits to be better utilized, the small-business owner was able to become more successful in a shorter period of time. Eventually, the idea of shared space and services caught on. As a result of the industry's growth and its quest for new information, the Executive Suite Association was developed. The ESA now holds educational and networking conferences across the country and the world.

The ________________, LLC has many great attributes. Our attractive and ideally located building is only a minute or so from Highway 36. This allows our clients convenient and easy access to Denver, Interlocken, Boulder and the surrounding areas. ESL's location is a perfect place for individuals who work closely with the area's hi-tech companies, as well as being in a wonderful environment. Our facility is a place that people want to come to work—and that starts with you! Your pleasant and helpful attitude will make the difference in our business.

HANDBOOK INTRODUCTION

This Handbook has been prepared as a guide to familiarize ________________, LLC EMPLOYEES with the overall employment policies and benefit programs of the company. The information contained in this handbook is for general information only. It will acquaint you with generalized descriptions of the policies, rules, pay and benefits that apply to your employment. Neither the Handbook nor the language that it contains directly or indirectly constitutes any form of employment contract between any employee and the company.

Employees who want more specific information may contact the General Manager.

Please read this handbook carefully and keep it handy for future reference. *It is your responsibility to be familiar with the contents of this handbook and any revisions or additions to it.*

Since our business is constantly changing, we expressly reserve the right to change any of our policies, including those covered here, at any time. Reasonable efforts will be made to keep you apprised of any changes in the policies and programs summarized in this handbook. However, the company reserves the right to amend, replace and/or terminate any or all of the policies and programs without prior notice to employees.

Use of the pronouns "he," "him," or "his" in this Handbook, to save repetition, will include and refer equally to the pronouns "she," "her," or "hers."

EQUAL OPPORTUNITY

The company maintains a policy of nondiscrimination with all employees and applicants for employment. All aspects of employment with us will be governed on the basis of merit, competence and qualifications and will not be influenced in any manner by race, religion, sex, age, national origin, disability, or any other basis prohibited by law.

All decisions made with respect to recruiting, hiring and promoting for a job will be based solely on individual qualifications related to the requirements of the position. Likewise, all other personnel matters—such as compensation, benefits, transfers, reduction-in-force, recall, and training—will be administered free from any illegal discriminatory practices.

EMPLOYMENT OF RELATIVES

We have no general prohibition against hiring relatives. However, a few restrictions have been established to help prevent problems of safety, security, supervision and morale.

While we accept and consider applications for employment from close family members—such as parents, children, spouses, or in-laws—they will not be hired in positions where they directly or indirectly supervise or are supervised by another close family member or where they have access to sensitive or confidential information regarding other close relatives.

DEFINITION OF EMPLOYMENT STATUS

The following terms will be used to describe the classification of employees and their employment status.

REGULAR

Employees who have completed the 90-day orientation period. Regular employees, like all employees of the company, are employed for an indefinite period of time and are employees-at-will.

FULL-TIME

Employees scheduled to work 40 hours per week. Full-time employees are eligible for all benefits when applicable service requirements are met.

PART-TIME

Employees scheduled to work less then 40 per week. Employees working less than 40 hours per week are not eligible for company benefits.

EXEMPT

Executive, managerial, administrative, and certain professional positions are considered "exempt" from coverage by the Fair Labor Standards Act (FLSA). Employees in exempt positions are paid a weekly salary for overall performance of a job and are not covered by FLSA requirements for overtime pay.

SALARIED NONEXEMPT

Employees whose positions do not meet FLSA exemption tests and who are paid a specified weekly salary to complete their job requirements. This weekly salary is protected at the 40-hours-per-week rate and the employee receives one-half times their regular rate of pay per hour worked in excess of 40 hours per week.

TEMPORARY

Employees who are hired for a pre-established period, usually during peak workloads or for vacation relief. They may work a full-time or part-time schedule. They are ineligible for company benefits and holiday pay.

All employees are employed for an indefinite period of time. The company retains the discretion to terminate the employment relationship at any time and for any reason.

CONTRACT

Contract employees have specific duties and compensation for a definite period of time. Contract employees may not be eligible for company benefits unless otherwise identified in the contract.

REFERENCE CHECKS

Company policy requires that the General Manager handle all requests for information regarding current or former employees.

If you receive a telephone call or written request for information regarding salary, work, performance, behavior, employment status, disciplinary action, employee interaction and relationship, or any other employee information, regarding yourself, another employee or a former employee, you must refer these requests to the General Manager.

It is not customary for the company to give reference letters to employees or prospective employers or former employees.

ORIENTATION PERIOD

During this period, which usually lasts approximately 90 days, a new employee is expected to learn his job and to reach an adequate level of performance. He should also use this time to determine whether or not the position adequately meets his own expectations and personal needs. He is expected to do the job he applied for and perform without exception those duties he agreed to do. Refer to page 22: '"Corrective Action."'

Periodically during the orientation period, the employee and his supervisor should get together to discuss the employee's progress and to identify areas in which additional training or effort may be required. These discussions are not meant to be one-sided. The employee should feel free to let the supervisor know of any ideas or concerns he has regarding the position or the organization and if there is a need for more frequent reviews or feedback.

You will not receive prorated vacation pay if you terminate during the initial orientation period or any extension thereof. Newly hired employees do not accrue vacation during the orientation period. After satisfactory completion of this period, vacation accrual is retroactive to the date of hire.

The first 90 days after a transfer or promotion within the company is also considered an orientation period. However, any existing benefits will remain in effect during this time.

PERSONNEL RECORDS

Important events in each employee's history with the company will be recorded and kept in the employee's personnel file. Performance reviews, change-of-status records, commendations, disciplinary warnings and educational attainment records are examples of records maintained.

Your personnel file is available for your inspection by making an appointment with the General Manager. Under no circumstances will personnel files be copied or removed from the General Manager's office.

Each employee is responsible for notifying the General Manager of changes in address, telephone number, and/or family status (births, marriage, death, divorce, legal separation, etc.). This responsibility includes employees on layoff status and leave of absence.

GENERAL WAGE AND BONUS POLICY

The ________________, LLC is committed to rewarding its employees via bonuses to non-contract employees. This will be done at the company's discretion to reward exceptional performance and to motivate employees to achieve a superior level of performance.

PAYCHECKS

Hours will be turned in every other Monday, and paychecks will be issued every other Friday. This cycle will then continue.

Paychecks not picked up on payday will be held by the General Manager until the employee is available to pick up the check or has made other arrangements with the General Manager. Upon employee's request, the paycheck may be mailed.

However, paychecks will not, under any circumstances, be released to anyone other than the employee.

EMPLOYEE ADVANCES

It is The ______________, LLC's policy to decline all requests for early paychecks or pay advances for personal reasons.

BUSINESS TRAVEL ADVANCES

In the case of business travel, The _______________, LLC will advance funds based on what is believed to be reasonable.

GARNISHMENTS

Upon receipt of a properly executed garnishment, a portion of your paycheck may be held until a court order is issued indicating satisfaction of indebtedness or until we are ordered to surrender the pay to the court or its agent. Garnishments are expensive and time consuming and should be avoided.

MISCELLANEOUS DEDUCTIONS

Other Payroll deductions may also be made at the employee's election for group insurance and other acceptable uses.

Please contact the General Manager if you have any questions about the Payroll-deduction services provided by the company.

SOCIAL SECURITY (FICA)

If you have any questions regarding Social Security benefits, please contact the General Manager.

CHARITABLE DONATIONS

The _______________, LLC is conscious of its and its employees' obligation to help others not as fortunate. The company will match up to $100 per year of any employee contribution to a recognized charity, subject to company approval.

Those desiring to take advantage of this policy should submit their check payable to the charity of their choice, to the General

Manager where it will be matched, up to the limit above, and forwarded to the designated recipient. To avoid disappointment, employees are encouraged to contact the General Manager in advance to determine what constitutes an approved charity.

From time to time, a payroll deduction plan may be offered for certain charities.

EMPLOYEE BENEFITS AND SERVICES

The company offers a package of employee benefit programs. *Because the company pays a major portion of the total cost, this "hidden paycheck" constitutes a large and valuable portion of your total compensation.*

Our group health-insurance program may be continued if you leave the company under circumstances described by Federal Law. The following descriptions of benefits are only brief summaries for your general information. Complete and official details of insurance and payroll plans can be obtained from the General Manager.

The existence of these employee benefits and plans, in and of themselves, does not signify that an employee will be employed for the requisite time necessary to qualify for these benefits and plans.

Reasonable efforts will be made to keep employees apprised of any changes in the benefits summarized below. However, the company reserves the right to amend, replace, and/or terminate any or all of the benefits without prior notice to employees.

In addition, all company benefit programs are explicitly defined in legal documents, including insurance contracts and official plan documents.

Should any question arise concerning the nature or extent of the program benefits, the formal language of the plan document or contract (and not the informal language of this Handbook or any other writing or verbal representation) must govern. Appropriate documents are available through the General Manager.

GROUP INSURANCE

The company makes available a comprehensive health and dental program for regular full-time employees who meet specific eligibility requirements and their dependents.

HEALTH INSURANCE

Your health coverage will become effective after a brief waiting period following your continuous, full-time employment. The company covers no less than 25% of the premium for the employee.

DENTAL INSURANCE

The company maintains a group dental-insurance plan. You become eligible for this at the same time that you become eligible for health insurance. The company covers no less then 25% of the premium for the employee.

DISABILITY

The ____________________, LLC presently does not offer a disability plan. Unknown illness and injuries may occur at any time, and employees are encouraged to explore such coverage as deemed necessary.

STATE UNEMPLOYMENT INSURANCE

If you have any questions regarding unemployment insurance, please contact the General Manager.

WORKERS' COMPENSATION

Report any work-related accidents or illness immediately to your supervisor and to the General Manager. Failure to report an accident that develops into a "lost time" accident at a later date could create difficulty in obtaining Workers' Compensation benefits. Belated injury claims may result in the claim's being denied.

Employees requiring medical attention will be referred to Boulder Community Hospital (Colorado). Any work-related injuries or illness requiring after-hours treatment should be taken to the nearest appropriate medical facility.

TIME CLOCKS

Time clocks are used by hourly employees to record their hours during a pay period. Your supervisor will train you in the use of the time clock.

Failure to punch in and/or out on a regular basis will result in disciplinary action. *Abuse of the time clock procedure will be grounds for dismissal.*

At times the honor system of keeping track of hours worked may be utilized. *If at any time it is discovered and proved that you turned in a false time sheet, immediate termination will take place.*

OVERTIME

Overtime pay will conform to provisions of the FLSA. The _______________, LLC requests that overtime work be avoided. All overtime work by nonexempt employees must be authorized in advance by your supervisor, who will be responsible for the period of the overtime.

LUNCH AND REST PERIODS

All employees receive either a half-hour or a one-hour unpaid lunch period based on daily hours worked. Employees are encouraged to take their lunch break each day. This period is to be coordinated and scheduled with your supervisor to ensure that all essential functions are covered. Employee will clock out during his lunch break. If lunch will be more than one hour, an employee is required to get prior approval from his supervisor. Disciplinary action may be taken for a pattern of employee abuse of the lunch-break privilege.

Employees may take two paid breaks per day, as work allows. Breaks can be *up to* five minutes in length. This break may not be combined with the employee's lunch period. Employees are encouraged to take their breaks away from their desks without disturbing the work of fellow employees or clients.

COMP TIME POLICY

If you are classified as a non-exempt employee, then you may take comp time in lieu of overtime. Comp time must be taken in the same workweek, which is defined as Monday through Sunday.

The only exception to this rule is if you work on a company holiday. In that case, you may substitute any other day for the missed holiday, with your supervisor's approval. Otherwise, the holiday will be considered part of the 40-hour workweek.

VACATIONS

All regular full-time employees who have completed *six calendar months* of continuous employment are eligible to take a paid vacation not to exceed total vacation hours accrued. Full-time employees (40 hours per week) will accrue vacation hours according to the following schedule:

LENGTH OF EMPLOYMENT

Completed:	Vacation Earned	Hours Earned Per Pay Period
1 Year	1 Week	1.54 Hours
2 Years	2 Weeks	3.08 Hours
5 Years	2.5 Weeks	3.84 Hours
8 Years	3 Weeks	4.61 Hours

Vacation must be scheduled with your supervisor. To satisfy your preference, as well as to meet the staffing needs of the company, discuss your vacation plans with your supervisor well in advance.

Temp-to-permanent employees begin accruing vacation time 90 days after becoming full-time regular employees.

Our vacation plan is designed to provide you with the opportunity to rest and get away from the everyday routine. Therefore, vacation should be taken annually to assure that you receive the full benefit of this plan.

Vacation time is not earned during sick leave or an unpaid leave of absence that exceeds 30 calendar days. None of the unused vacation time for the current year will be paid upon *termination* from ESL or upon employee quitting without 2 weeks notice. Pay will be computed based on the rate earned upon termination.

The "Vacation Year" will begin on December 1 and end November 30. Any unused vacation time at the end of the year will be bought back at half the wage currently being paid by The ________________, LLC. Vacations may not be accrued from year to year, except that one week can be carried over into the year following the year in which it was earned, at your option.

* Vacation cannot exceed more then 2 weeks in consecutive order unless authorized by ESL.

HOLIDAYS

Full-time regular employees who have completed 30 days with The ________________, LLC are eligible for the six paid holidays each calendar year. However, if the 90-day orientation is not completed and the employee is terminated for any reason, the employee owes The ________________, LLC any holiday pay received during the orientation period.

To receive holiday pay, *you must work the regularly scheduled workday before and after the holiday, unless an exception is approved in writing or the holiday falls during a scheduled vacation.* A paid holiday does not count as a day worked in calculating overtime for the week.

The following are the six company-paid holidays:

- New Year's Day — January 1
- Memorial Day — Last Monday in May
- Independence Day — July 4
- Thanksgiving Day — Fourth Thursday in November
- Labor Day — First Monday in September
- Christmas Day — December 25

Employees may be eligible for two additional paid holidays as follows:
- Day after Thanksgiving, Fourth Friday in November
- Christmas Eve, December 24

To qualify for the day after Thanksgiving and/or Christmas Eve Day as paid holidays, the employee must be a regular, full-time employee who has completed *six calendar months* of continuous employment and has worked the regularly scheduled day before and after the holiday.

Paid holidays that fall on a Saturday will normally be observed on the preceding Friday; holidays that fall on a Sunday will normally be observed on the following Monday. If a holiday falls during your vacation, it may be added to your vacation or used in place of vacation hours. If you terminate or begin an unpaid leave of absence on the last workday preceding a holiday, then you will not receive holiday pay.

LEAVE OF ABSENCE WITH PAY

BEREAVEMENT LEAVE

In the event of death in your immediate family, you may have time needed up to 3 working days with pay to handle family affairs and attend the funeral. Immediate family is defined as father, mother, brother, sister, spouse, child, daughter or son-in-law, mother or father-in-law, grandparents or grandchild.

For absence due to the death of a relative other than a member of the immediate family, you will be allowed one day of absence with pay.

This benefit is not available if the time off occurs while you were away from work because of vacation, designated or floating holiday, sickness (paid or unpaid) or any other reason.

JURY DUTY

In order that you may serve on a jury without loss of earnings, the company will pay the difference between your regular earnings and the fee you receive for jury service for all regular full-time employees who have completed their orientation period. You must contact your supervisor and the General Manager immediately upon receiving notification to appear.

While serving on a jury, you will be expected to work as much of your regular hours as the jury schedule permits, to the extent that combined time on the jury and at work does not exceed 40 hours in any given week, if you are a nonexempt employee. For contract employees, compensation will still be paid as scheduled. Record your jury duty time on your time sheet and present the official court check or other documentation of remuneration to payroll in order to receive the difference between your regular wages and jury compensation.

LEAVE OF ABSENCE WITHOUT PAY

We recognize that occasionally events such as birth or adoption, a serious health condition, personal reason or military orders can occur that would require a temporary absence from work. Under certain circumstances, leaves of absence can be approved which would protect some or all of your employment rights.

If your work site employs 50 or more people within 75 miles (some state laws may vary) and you meet the eligibility requirements, absence for birth, adoption, or serious health condition fall under the jurisdiction of the Family and Medical Leave Act (FMLA) and will be administered accordingly.

If your work site employs fewer then 50 people within 75 miles, or you do not meet the eligibility requirements for FMLA, medical and maternity leave may be granted under the Medical Leave Policy.

FMLA LEAVE

Up to 12 workweeks (some state laws may vary) for reasons prescribed under the law. Details of the Family and Medical Leave Act may be obtained from the General Manager. To be eligible, you must have been employed for a minimum of 12 months and have worked at least 1,250 hours. Employees have the duty to give 30 days notice of intent to take FMLA leave for foreseeable events.

MEDICAL LEAVE

Up to 4 workweeks for employees who are unable to work due to non-occupational illness or injury when supported by a physician's statement. During the first two weeks of leave, any accrued vacation and sick time must be used. During the course of medical leave, it is your responsibility to keep your supervisor informed as to your status and condition. Failure to maintain such contact on a regular basis could result in the loss of approved leave status or as prescribed by law.

PERSONAL LEAVE

May range from 5-30 consecutive days for compelling personal reasons. To be eligible, you must have maintained a satisfactory record of employment for a minimum of one year. Approval is made at the discretion of your supervisor with the concurrence of one higher level of management. **Personal leave is a privilege, not a right, and is earned through service and good record or attendance and performance.** Requests will be reviewed in light of the length of time you will be away, the effect the leave will have on your coworkers' ability to carry out their responsibilities, your position and your length of employment.

MILITARY LEAVE

An employee who volunteers or is called to active military duty in a branch of the US Armed Forces will be granted a leave of absence in accordance with state and federal law for the period of active duty.

While on leave for the National Guard or Reserve, The _______________, LLC will pay the difference between the amount paid by the respective armed serves branch and the employee's regular wage for up to two weeks per year.

VOTING

The _________________, LLC encourages all employees to vote. Employees are encouraged to use their hours off to vote. If this cannot be arranged, then your supervisor can approve time off to vote at an appropriate time either at the beginning or end of the work day, provided at least 48 hours notice is given.

LEAVE NOTIFICATION

You must notify the General Manager at least 2 weeks prior to the end of your leave of your availability to return to work if you have been absent more then 30 days. You may be required to have a physical examination to determine your fitness for work prior to your return. Failure to return may be considered a voluntary resignation. Acceptance of employment while on leave or falsification of a request for extension will be grounds for termination. Benefits such as holidays, vacation, and sick time will not accrue during a leave of absence. For information regarding group-insurance coverage during your leave, contact the General Manager.

Details regarding reinstatement following an unpaid leave of absence are available in the General Manager's office.

CONDUCT

Professional standards of office etiquette are to be observed at all times. Personal contact with visitors, clients, and callers should always be pleasant and businesslike. People associate our company with the person with whom they have direct contact. **Remember, first impressions are lasting impressions.**

Employees are also asked to be courteous in their dealings with each other. A professional and friendly atmosphere will help to make a pleasant work place.

Employees should refrain from developing intimate relationships with individuals in the following categories: 1) Our Clients: either individuals or employees of companies that pay the Company for space and/or services. 2) Our Clients' Clients or Vendors: those individuals or employees of companies that pay or are otherwise associated with our client. 3) Our Vendors: those individuals or employees of companies providing goods or services to the company.

Becoming close (beyond normal working relationships) with a client can cause conflict of interest and may alter your ability to make sound judgments. Employees who become intimately involved with a client, vendor, or other individuals who are remotely associated with The ________________, LLC will be disciplined and possibly terminated.

EMPLOYEE NONDISCLOSURE AGREEMENTS

When you joined the company, you were required to sign a Nondisclosure Agreement concerning inventions, trade secrets, conflict of interest, confidentiality, confidential information and computer security. By signing this document, you agreed not to discuss proprietary information, inside or outside of the company. If you have any questions about this document, you may discuss them with the General Manager.

INCOMPLETE AGREEMENTS

Any agreement or other document not containing original signatures will be returned to the appropriate individuals prior to processing.

Any forged signatures will be immediate grounds for dismissal.

RESIGNATION

If you decide to leave the company, please advise your supervisor or the General Manager in writing 2 weeks prior to your date of departure so that an orderly transition can be made. This process includes turning in company property and obtaining appropriate clearances.

EXIT INTERVIEW

At the time of termination, The General Manager will conduct an exit interview.

RETURN OF COMPANY PROPERTY

Terminated employees are responsible for returning all company property—including keys, tools, files, manuals, etc.—prior to actual termination. Final payment of wages, action pay, etc., may be withheld pending return of company property.

REINSTATEMENT

Employees who terminate a position with the company and rehire within 30 calendar days will be fully reinstated to all insurance and accrued benefits they had accumulated prior to the resignation. Reinstatement of insurance and benefits, however, may require payment of back premiums.

Employees who are terminated for reasons beyond their control, such as a reduction in force, and are hired within 3 months of the date they were terminated, will have their previous hire date reinstated. Full details are available from the General Manager.

Employees who voluntarily terminate a position and are rehired after a period of 30 days will be considered new employees.

EMPLOYEE SAFETY AND HEALTH

We make every effort to provide safe working conditions for our employees. We observe the safety laws of the governmental bodies within whose jurisdiction we operate. No one will knowingly be required to work in any unsafe manner. Safety is every employee's responsibility. All employees are requested to do everything reasonable and necessary to keep the company a safe place to work. You are responsible for becoming acquainted with safety guidelines and for observing these guidelines at all times.

In addition, all employees are requested to immediately report any unsafe or hazardous work-place condition directly to a supervisor. Employees are also requested to report any occurrence that the employee believes could create a hazardous or unsafe condition in the work place.

Employees working after dark are asked to park their cars in the front lot south of the building. This area offers better night lighting and security.

LIFE-THREATENING ILLNESS

We are committed to providing fair and equal opportunity to all employees, including those who have a life-threatening illness. We are also committed to providing a safe work environment that meets or exceeds state and federal regulations. Consequently, employees who have a life-threatening illness will be treated like other employees as long as they meet performance standards and medical and other evidence indicates their condition does not present a threat to others or an increased threat to themselves in the work place.

We also believe all information regarding an employee with a life-threatening illness must remain private and confidential. We ask all employees to treat employees with a life-threatening illness with compassion and understanding.

SUBSTANCE ABUSE

The ________________, LLC recognizes that substances such as alcohol and drugs are used by individuals, sometimes to an extent that their abilities and senses are impaired. Our position regarding substance abuse is the same whether alcohol, marijuana, illegal drugs, prescription drugs, or controlled substances are involved.

The employee who begins work (at the corporate office or anywhere an employee may be conducting business for The ________________, LLC) while impaired or who becomes impaired while at work is guilty of a major violation of company rules and is subject to severe disciplinary action.

Severe disciplinary action can include suspension, dismissal, or any other penalty appropriate under the circumstances. Likewise, the use, possession, transfer, or sale of any substance on company premises, in any company business elsewhere is prohibited; and violations are subject to severe disciplinary action. The ________________, LLC may also notify appropriate authorities, after appropriate investigation by the supervisor or a company officer.

The ________________, LLC has resources available to assist an employee who requests help with substance abuse. Employees who are placed in a rehabilitation program because of performance or behavior problems due to substance abuse are subject to dismissal for failure to successfully complete the program or change their performance or behavior.

Applicants who have a past history of substance abuse and who can provide medical assurance of acceptable control may be considered for employment with ________________, LLC as long as they are otherwise qualified for the position for which they are applying.

Alcoholic beverages shall not be served or used on The ________________, LLC premises at any time without the express consent of the Company. Social activities held off premises and paid for on a personal basis are not affected by this policy.

As long as employee information is not needed for police or security purposes, The ________________, LLC shall maintain employee medical and personnel information in confidence and release this information to authorized company personnel on a "need to know" basis. An exception to this policy is when the employee signs a release for the transfer of such information.

SMOKING

In view of the serious consequences of smoking on the health of employees and in order to protect sensitive electronic equipment, the company deems it important that employees refrain from smoking except in designated areas outside of the building.

Employees who smoke may step outside during their breaks and lunchtime to the areas provided.

Please do not use the front-entrance area or front walk as a smoking area. Use the ashtrays provided and do not litter the walkways.

ACCIDENTS

No matter how insignificant an injury may seem at the time of occurrence, you must immediately notify your supervisor and the General Manager. We are committed to working diligently and conscientiously to eliminate unsafe conditions. This aim can be achieved only if all employees cooperate by identifying and eliminating such conditions. The prevention of work-related injuries is of such importance that it should be given precedence over operating productivity.

Supervisors are responsible for completing the **Accident Investigation Form** available from the General Manager.

Employees requiring medical attention will be referred to Boulder Community Hospital. Any work-related injuries or illnesses requiring after-hours treatment should be taken to the nearest appropriate facility.

Please note that if you are involved in a work-related accident or injury where employee negligence is a factor, then you may be required to submit to a substance-abuse test.

SAFE DRIVING RECORD

In order to ensure the safety of company employees and equipment, and to protect the interest of the company, the following applies to all employees who operate company-owned or hired vehicles or who operate personal vehicles for company business:

1. The company's insurance agent may request semiannually a DMV report on all employees who operate company-owned vehicles. If your record indicates more than 2 minor violations within the past 2 years, you may not be permitted to operate these vehicles and you may be subject to disciplinary measures up to and including termination.
2. You must possess a valid license to drive. If, for any reason, this license is suspended, revoked or expired, then you must immediately cease operating said vehicles.
3. All employees are required to wear seat belts while operating or riding in said vehicles.

All employees who operate company-owned or hired vehicles or who operate personal vehicles while conducting company business are expected to do so in a safe manner, obeying all traffic rules and regulations. In accordance with state and federal law, no employee will operate said vehicles while under the influence of alcohol or illegal drugs. Doing so will subject you to disciplinary measures up to and including termination.

VEHICLE ACCIDENT REPORTING

If you are involved in an accident, regardless of how minor, while driving a company-owned or hired vehicle or while driving your personal vehicle while conducting business, the police must be notified and a report filed. As soon as practical, notify the General Manager so that the appropriate insurance claim can be filed.

Disciplinary action will be initiated if you fail to notify the General Manager of any vehicle accident. If another party is involved, instruct him to contact the insurance company listed in vehicle documents.

Obtain a copy of the police report and submit it to the General Manager.

AUTHORIZATION TO OPERATE VEHICLES

Unless specifically authorized by a company officer, if you are provided a company-owned vehicle, you are not authorized to allow anyone who is not an employee of the company to operate that vehicle. This includes members of your family, subcontractors, friends, or acquaintances. If you hire a vehicle for company use, you must designate on the rental agreement who will be covered under the company or rental insurance policies. You could find yourself responsible for the cost of repairs as well as being subject to disciplinary action up to and including termination.

If you operate an employee-owned vehicle on company business, you must maintain adequate personal liability and property-damage insurance coverage, and provide to the company a certificate from your insurance company listing The ________________, LLC as "Additional Insured." The company does not provide insurance that covers the loss of personal property.

The driver and any passengers must wear seat belts at all times. *It is recommended that you take a break or switch drivers every two hours during an extended period of travel.*

GENERAL STANDARDS

Groups of people who are working together for any purpose require certain guidelines pertaining to their conduct and relationships. Accordingly, our employees must be aware of their responsibilities to the company and to coworkers.

We intend to take a constructive approach to disciplinary matters to ensure that action that would interfere with operations or an employee's job is not continued.

Although there is no way to identify every possible violation of standards of conduct, the following is a partial list of infractions that will result in disciplinary action or termination:

1. Falsification of company records—including but not limited to employment application, client files, expense reports or time reporting.
2. Unauthorized possession of company or employee property, fraud, gambling, carrying weapons or explosives, or violation of criminal laws on company premises.
3. Fighting, throwing things, horseplay, practical jokes or other disorderly conduct which may endanger the well-being of any employee or company operation.
4. Threatening, intimidating, coercing, using abusive language, or interfering with the performance of fellow employees.
5. Insubordination or refusal to comply with instructions or failure to perform reasonable duties to which assigned.
6. Use of company material, time or equipment for the manufacture or production of an article for unauthorized purposes or personal use.
7. Conduct that the company feels reflects adversely on the employee or company.
8. Performance that, in the company's opinion, does not meet the requirements of the position.

9. Engaging in such other practices as may be inconsistent with the ordinary and reasonable rules of conduct necessary to the welfare of the company and its employees, including theft from employees, vendors or clients.
10. Discussing employee compensation, including rate of pay and bonuses.
11. Willful or repeated violations of safety rules.
12. Use, possession, sale, purchase, transfer or being under the influence of alcoholic beverages, illegal drugs or other intoxicants at any time on company premises or while on company business. “Company premises” is defined as office space, warehouse space, any company housing, owned or leased, and all customers’ premises.
13. Misusing, damaging or destroying the property of others or company property.
14. Consciously making materials misrepresentations to other employees, clients, or management.
15. Performing other activities for which the company feels that discipline is warranted.

This list is intended to be representative of the types of activities that may result in disciplinary action. It is not intended to be comprehensive and does not alter the employment-at-will relationship between the employee and company.

Additional standards of conduct are described in the next sections.

ATTENDANCE STANDARDS

Punctuality and regular attendance are essential to the proper operations of any business. They also help you to establish a good working reputation and add to your opportunity for advancement.

If you are unable to report to work for any reason, notify your supervisor (or, in his absence, the General Manager) before starting time.

We reserve the right to require a physician's release when an employee returns to work following a disability or serious injury.

If an employee is late to work (after the agreed starting time) more than two times in a 10-week time period, then the employee will be given a written warning. Repeated occurrences will result in dismissal at the General Manager's discretion.

ABSENCE WITHOUT NOTICE

For us to operate our business effectively, we ask that you keep us informed of your status when you are off work because of illness or accident from any cause. If you fail to notify us after two consecutive days of absence, then we will presume that you have resigned and you will be removed from the Payroll. If you must leave work for any reason before the end of your scheduled shift, you must inform your supervisor.

If your absence is planned, please notify your supervisor as soon as possible to allow proper coverage of your responsibilities.

HARASSMENT, INCLUDING SEXUAL HARASSMENT

The _________________, LLC will not tolerate any form of harassment in the work environment, including sexual harassment. Because sexual harassment interferes with work performance; creates an intimidating, hostile, or offensive work environment; influences or tends to affect the career, salary, working conditions, responsibilities, duties and other aspects of career development of an employee or prospective employee; and creates an explicit or implicit term or condition of an individual's employment, it will not be tolerated.

Sexual harassment, as defined in this handbook, includes but is not limited to sexual advances, verbal or physical conduct of a sexual nature (e.g., signs, posters, and the like), requests for sexual favors, any conditioning of tangible employee benefits upon submission to sexual conduct, and any conduct that has the purpose of unreasonably interfering with an employee's work performance or creating a hostile or offensive working environment.

All employees are requested to immediately report any suspected harassment, including harassment based on age, of which they are aware to a corporate officer or to the General Manager. A prompt and confidential investigation will be conducted and corrective actions will be taken against those found to have engaged in harassing conduct or those found to have made false complaints.
Supervisors have an additional responsibility to avoid even the appearance of impropriety in relations with other employees.

OUTSIDE EMPLOYMENT

If you have another job or are thinking of taking one, then you must discuss it with your supervisor or team leader to ensure you avoid the following:

1. Work for a subcontractor, customer, or vendor that could place you in a position of conflict of interest. This could lead to immediate dismissal.
2. Working for a competitor, if you have access to proprietary or confidential information.

If you accept outside employment, then you must be aware that as a full-time employee of the company, you still will be expected to completely meet all requirements of your company job.

COMPLAINT-HANDLING PROCEDURE

Under normal conditions, if you have a job-related problem, question or complaint, then you should discuss it with your supervisor. The simplest, quickest and most satisfactory solution will often be reached at this level.

CONFIDENTIALITY

During the course of your employment here, you will be working with our customer list, business systems, future plans, client data and other information that we consider confidential. Maintaining its confidentiality is essential to our competitive position in the industry and, ultimately, to our ability to achieve financial success and provide employment stability. Protect this information by safeguarding it when in use, filing it properly when not being used, and discussing it only with those who have a legitimate business need to know. You will be asked to sign a Nondisclosure Agreement intended to protect the confidentiality of proprietary information.

Employees may come in contact with personal and sensitive information regarding clients. It should be understood that employees are expected to represent the company with the highest professional standards of integrity and that this sensitive information should be kept in strict confidence within the office and not be discussed with or disclosed to others outside the company.

The company has incurred considerable expense to develop unique methods of organizing and implementing its systems, procedures and services. Employees may receive certain confidential information and other trade secrets concerning the operation, methods, systems, and procedures that should not be discussed with or disclosed to others outside the company. Employees are required to abide by the terms and conditions of the Nondisclosure Agreement and confidentiality provisions of agreement that they sign, including the duty to report any unauthorized disclosure of confidential information of which they are aware.

Employees are reminded that these agreements remain in effect after any termination of the employment relationship.

SECURITY

Employees are expected to be concerned about security at all times.

Information security is an important concern for the company. All information is made available only on a need-to-know basis. This is to protect employees from unnecessary liability and to prevent harm to the company or its customers. No employee is to view or modify information unless he has received specific authority and his job function requires such access. No employee is to share his computer long-on, building access code or password information with anyone, nor is anyone to attempt to defeat or circumvent any security feature of any system. All actual or potential security violations should be reported to a supervisor.

Office employees are issued procedures regarding security access and safety in the corporate office during off hours. Employees are requested to follow these procedures and to prevent their disclosure to any unauthorized parties.

E-MAIL

The electronic mail system is provided to expedite *business* communication among employees and with appropriate outside parties. It is not intended as a social chat line and should not be used as such. Employees are encouraged to use the e-mail system but are also encouraged to use other forms of communication when they are more appropriate or expedient. All employees using the e-mail system are requested to follow established procedures. All information sent or received by e-mail should be treated as confidential information and should be protected from disclosure to outside parties, except for those who have a need to know about the information. Employees are reminded that there may be a permanent record of all mail messages sent and received.

Derogatory comments and harassing or offensive language should never be used on the e-mail system.

Office employees are asked to check their e-mail messages every hour and non-corporate employees are asked to check their e-mail messages at least twice a day during regular business hours. **The e-mail system is subject to monitoring at any time with or without notice.**

TELEPHONE/P.A. SYSTEM

Telephones are an important part of the ______________, LLC business, and telephone conduct directly reflects the company's image and reputation. All employees are expected to maintain an appropriate level of courtesy and professionalism during telephone conversations at all times with any party. An employee should never use offensive language or tone or raise his voice when speaking on the telephone. Employees are asked to refrain from using speakerphones unless they are necessary.

Telephones in each station and office are intended for company business. The company recognizes that from time to time emergencies arise and personal business may need to be taken care of. However, the number and duration of personal calls should be kept to an absolute minimum. Personal long-distance calls at the company's expense are not authorized and will be deducted from each employee's paycheck. Personal long-distance calls may be grounds for termination.

CORRECTIVE ACTION

The company desires to protect its investment of time and expense devoted to employee orientation and training. Corrective action may be initiated when management believes that an employee's performance problem can be resolved through adequate counseling. Corrective actions are completely at the discretion of company management. If corrective counseling is implemented, then it may be terminated at the discretion of management. Management may either warn, reassign, suspend, or discharge any employee "at will," whichever it chooses and at any time. *Employees generally will be given two opportunities to correct any issues, after which the employee will be terminated due to failure to follow procedures as explained in person, in writing, and in this handbook.*

DRESS CODE

Employees should dress neatly in professional attire appropriate for contact with clients, visitors and vendors during normal business hours, from 8:30 a.m. until 5 p.m., Monday through Friday.

Jeans (any color), shorts, T-shirts, sweatshirts, tennis shoes, and hiking boots are typically not acceptable during the business week. For safety reasons, employees must wear shoes when walking throughout the office area. Visible body piercing (with the exception of ears) and tattoos, as well as extreme hair coloring, are not acceptable.

Employees meeting the public on behalf of The ________________, LLC business, off company premises, must be especially attentive to their appearance and should always be dressed appropriately.

All material is subject to change at any time. Changes will be given to all employees in writing.

Non-Disclosure Agreement.

AGREEMENT AS TO EMPLOYMENT

In consideration of my employment by the ______________, LLC, (the "Company") I, __________________ hereby agree to the following:

1. I will forever keep secret, confidential, and inviolate and never disclose, either during or after my employment by the Company, any proprietary or confidential information or business secret of the Company, including, without limitation, those relating (a) to the business, conduct or operations of the Company or of any of their respective clients, customers, consultants, or licensees; or (b) to any material, apparatus, processed, methods, ways of business, programs and/or formulae, etc., used in the production, development, manufacture, use, sale, or marketing of the Company's products or services. Upon leaving the employ of the Company for any reason, I shall promptly return to the Company all processes, formulae, drawings, notes, programs, plans,

models, customer lists or other records, reports, proposals, technical information, and reproduction thereof, that relate in any way to the Company's operations, business, assets, research, development work, or any of the foregoing items covered by this paragraph.

2. At no time during the term of my employment by the Company, and for a period of ONE YEAR thereafter, will I directly or indirectly, as an individual proprietor, partner, stockbroker, officer, director, joint venturer, investor, lender, employee, or in any capacity whatsoever (other than as the holder of a non-controlling investment in any publicly traded securities in the United States) compete with the business of the Company. As used herein, "compete" or "competition," or any variation thereof, shall mean any engagement or participating in, or furnishing aid or assistance in connection with, the distribution, sale, marketing, or rendering of products or services of the type and kind distributed, sold, marketed or rendered by the Company in the market areas set forth in the rider to this Agreement.

3. At no time during the term of my employment and for a period of TWO YEARS thereafter will I directly or indirectly (a) recruit, solicit, divert, or employ any present employee or independent contractor of the Company; (b) solicit, serve or divert any present customer of the Company or; (c) take any action or do anything that impairs or damages the business, prospects or goodwill of the Company.

4. Although I believe the restrictions contained herein are reasonable to protect business activity, time and geographic areas, in the event any court of competent jurisdiction deems any provision hereof to be unreasonable, then such restrictions will nevertheless remain effective but shall be considered amended as to such protected business activity, time or areas (or any one of them, as the case may be) as may be considered to be reasonable by such court, and as so amended shall be enforced. I, ____________________, hereby represent and warrant that my training, education and background are such that my ability to earn a livelihood shall not be impaired by virtue of this agreement.

5. In the event of my breach of any of the covenants herein contained, although the company's damage will be substantial, the same will be extremely difficult or impossible to ascertain, and money damages will not afford an adequate remedy. Therefore, in the event of any such breach, in addition to such other remedies that may be provided by law, the Company shall have the right to specific performance of the covenants herein contained by way of temporary and/or permanent injunctive relief, all as it elects.

6. All of my obligations arising under this Agreement shall survive the termination of my employment, regardless of the manner of such termination, and shall be binding upon my heirs, executors and administrators.

7. As used herein, the terms "employ," "employment," and words of similar import are used generally to refer to my association with the Company whereby I

render certain services and the Company pays me certain monies. I acknowledge that I may, in fact, render such services as an independent contractor and that by reason of this Agreement I have acquired no rights or privileges in addition to those granted by law to a person who performs the services that I render. I specifically acknowledge that this Agreement does not obligate the Company to continue to employ me in any capacity for any period of time.

8. The terms of any rider attached hereto are incorporated herein by reference.

Executed under seal as of the day and year written below:

Date: ___________________________

Employee Name: ______________________________

Employee Signature: ___________________________

Accepted By: _________________________________

EMPLOYEE ACKNOWLEDGMENT

By my signature below, I acknowledge that I have read the Employee Handbook. I understand and agree that the Handbook is not a contract nor is it a guarantee of employment for any specific period of time either expressed or implied. I understand that I, like all other non-contract employees of the Company, am an employee-at-will. This means that I may quit my employment with the Company at any time for any reason, just as the Company may terminate my employment at any time for any reason. I understand that this employment-at-will status may not be changed by any written or oral statement by an employee or officers of the Company and that the policies of the Handbook may be modified and changed from time to time at the sole discretion of the Company.

I, ____________________, have agreed to perform the duties and services of
____________________, Monday through Friday, from 8:30 a.m. to 5 p.m., as outlined below:

General duties to include the above schedule as well as the following: answering and directing phone calls in a friendly, happy and professional tone; greeting all guests to the facility in a friendly, happy, professional tone; sorting mail; assisting clients as directed by the Company; cleaning up the facility as directed by the Company; assisting the Company in general as directed by management, as well as duties outlined in the Handbook or attending training workbooks as directed by the Company. The time and days listed above may need to be expanded from time to time in order for me to complete my duties; in such a case the Company will pay in accordance to the Handbook. Duties may change at any time at the sole discretion of the company.

____

Signature

____

Date

____

Print Name

V

Resources

The following may prove useful for in-depth information on some of the topics covered in this book, as well as other facets of operating a business. There are many others. Ask, and ye shall receive:

U. S. Small Business Administration—Check out their website —www.sba.gov. Your taxes are paying for this service, so you might as well see if there's anything you can use. Seriously, there's a ton of stuff, dealing with almost any phase of business you can think of. Time spent with some of their local people could pay off. Check to see if you could benefit from SCORE (Service Corps of Retired Executives).

Is there a local business school or college offering business courses? You might be able to get advice from some of the faculty or find an undergraduate or a graduate student intern willing to work with you.

The Wall Street Journal—I've seldom missed an issue in the last thirty years, as you might gather from the numerous quotes and references in this book. It's not just stock-market tables. The

Journal's writers cover many subjects of interest, no matter what your field of endeavor. I strongly suggest that you order a reprint of a special report that ran on October 28, 2002, if it is still available. It's entitled "The Company They Keep" and includes articles on The Employees, The Suppliers, The Investors, The Customers, and The Family. It's an extended "Milking Stool" and well worth reading. You can call the *Journal* office at 1-800-Journal to ask about it.

Your state's commerce department—In Colorado, it's the Secretary of State. Especially helpful in getting organized and dealing with your taxes and reporting. I noted a sign on a storefront recently offering incorporation service for $300. You can do it yourself in Colorado, with forms, over the Net for $50. Takes maybe a half-hour to download and complete the forms.

Your local Chamber of Commerce—Their mission is helping businesses in your area.

Nolo Press—This company publishes a number of informative, reasonably-priced business-oriented books—www.nolo.com.

Bloomberg Press—Another good source for business books.

www.bizmove.com—An amazing source of all kinds of free (and not free) information specifically aimed at the new and growing small businessperson.

The Web in general. With a little effort, you can find information on almost any subject. Rather than retyping Kipling's poem "If" for the Appendix, I found it on a website and just pressed COPY and PASTE.

Local and national business associations, such as Rotary, Toastmasters, etc.—There are also organizations at which the members swap leads.

The Internal Revenue Service—www.irs.gov—You can download most forms and instructions. They will send you a free CD, which contains information to help keep you out of trouble.

Your state's revenue department, which you can probably find on the Web.

Bibliography

This is a list of books, both the ones consulted specifically while researching this book and those that I can remember, that have proven useful in years past. I have marked with an asterisk those that you might find especially helpful to augment the material in this book. When I looked at Amazon's site, I found a ton of books on just about every topic in this book. I'm sure a lot of them are worthwhile. I did my reading on the plane, while in customers' waiting rooms, and at night, in hotels.

* Carnegie, Dale, et al: *How to Win Friends and Influence People*, Pocket Books

Gates, Bill: *Business @ the Speed of Thought*, Warner Books

Gates, Bill: *The Road Ahead*, Viking

* Girard, Joe: *How to Sell Anything to Anybody*, Warner Books

* Jacobs, Deborah L.: *Small Business Legal Smarts*, Bloomberg Press

* Johnson, Spencer, M.D., and Wilson, Larry: *The One-Minute Salesperson*, William Morrow

Lowe, Janet: *Warren Buffett Speaks*, John Wiley & Sons

* Mackay, Harvey and Blanchard, Kenneth: *Swim with the Sharks Without Being Eaten Alive*, Ballentine Books

* Malburg, Christopher R., CPA, MBA: *Accounting for the New Business*, Adams Media Corp

* Ruggero, Ed: *Duty First*, Harper Collins
* Stolze, William J.: *Start Up*, 5th Edition, Career Press
* Traverso, Debra Koontz, et al: *The Small Business Owner's Guide to a Good Night's Sleep*, Bloomberg Press
* Turner, Marcia Layton: *The Unofficial Guide to Starting a Small Business*, IDG Books Worldwide (This might be worthwhile for the copies of forms and the huge list of resources at the end.)

Welch, Jack: *Jack: Straight from the Gut*, Warner Business Books
* Ziglar, Zig: *Secrets of Closing the Sale*, Berkley Publishing Group

Thanks

Thanks to the troops at Skylark Bowl, The Tetra Company, High Country Trails, Careful Appliance, Bancard, Inc., and Louisville Executive Suites, who taught me many valuable lessons. Going back even further, thanks to the long-suffering real troops of the 603rd A.C. & W. Squadron, USAF, and the Illinois Air National Guard Communications Squadron. Finally, thanks to the people I tried to "supervise" in the various jobs I held prior to starting off on my own. Sorry for many of the dumb things I said and did. I hope I didn't make your lives too miserable.

Thanks to Josh Klein, one of the good lawyers, whose pro bono advice on a couple of delicate references in this book may have kept me out of court.

Special thanks to Judy Hearst, who put up with many years of, "You like to eat, don't you?" when she felt I was putting the company before all else.

Thanks also to Steve Hearst, who gave me the idea for this book, kept on my butt to get on with it, and patiently performed the initial editing task. At last, a return on four years of Harvard with an English major!

Thanks to Julie Hearst, M.B.A., who contributed much of the material on marketing.

Jay Hearst is involved in several business ventures in Colorado and Tennessee. He lives outside of Boulder with his wife, Judy, three horses, and three dogs.

Steve Hearst is a writer in Los Angeles. He lives with his wife, Julie, and his new daughter, Katie.

Let Jay Hearst Inspire and Enlighten Your Group

Would your organization or group benefit from the insights and advice of a been-there-done-that entrepreneur? If so, get ready for a truly memorable experience. Author Jay Hearst brilliantly brings the ideas in this book to life in a dynamic, inspiring presentation. Engage his speaking services and you will learn:

- Why starting your own business can be a path to unbelievable success, whether you're a Harvard MBA, a graduate of the School of Hard Knocks, or both.

- How to bypass the most common entrepreneurial mistakes and get started on the right foot.

- The identity of *the* most important factor in the success of any business—and how to make sure it's working for you.

- How to use Hearst's "Milking Stool" model to create and maintain a strong, steady foundation for your company.

- What you can do to maintain firm control over the financial/bookkeeping end of your business.

- How to nurture the "2s" in your company, those employees who make up the bulk of your work force—and what to do with the "1s" and the "3s."

- The fine art of transitioning from hands-on-everything entrepreneur to leader of a growing, thriving, mature company.

Interested? Call Jay Hearst at (303) 884-7788 for rates, scheduling information, and more details on how his life experience can help entrepreneurs start and operate successful, rewarding ventures.

ABOUT THE AUTHOR:

Jay Hearst is a been-there-done-that entrepreneur who has started, nurtured, and profited from several businesses, including one originally capitalized at $3,000 and sold, seventeen years later, for $60,000,000. He has been involved in a number of diverse fields, including credit card processing, horseback trail riding, hospital supplies, sales and marketing, and real estate. Some attempts have worked out better than others, but he has been right more than 50 percent of the time. He has learned from the successes as well as the others. He is currently involved in several business ventures in Colorado and Tennessee. Though he holds a degree from Harvard, Hearst maintains that his *other* degree—the one from the School of Hard Knocks—has taught him more about business and life…and these are the lessons he hopes to share with others.

www.ingramcontent.com/pod-product-compliance
Lightning Source LLC
LaVergne TN
LVHW091036080826
845145LV00002B/515

* 9 7 8 0 9 7 4 7 6 6 7 0 6 *